Learn
A Guide for Getting Started

Brian G. Burton, Ed.D.

Learning Lua: A Guide for Getting Started
By Brian G. Burton, Ed.D.

ISBN eBook: 978-1-937336-10-3
       Paperback: 978-1-937336-24-0
       (Paperback - Amazon): 979-8-857767-29-0
       (Hardback - Amazon):   979-8-859139-56-9

Version 1.0.0803.05 (8/2025)

Table of Contents

About the Author

Brian Gene Burton, Ed.D. is a professor, author, and game developer. He has written several textbooks, including "Learning Mobile App Development with Corona", "Creating Multiplayer Games with Unity 3D", and has contributed to several academic books on serious games and learning in virtual worlds. Dr. Burton teaches game development and virtual production and has an active YouTube station (https://www.youtube.com/@profburton). Dr. Burton presents and publishes his research internationally and enjoys sharing what he has learned.

Dedication

I dedicate this book to my loving wife whose support and encouragement kept me focused and writing. Thank you for keeping me focused and not running off on rabbit trails!

Preface

Who This Book Is For

While my focus and impetus for writing this book is that it be used as a textbook, I have also written it with the understanding that many (hopefully) are just interested in learning more about the Lua scripting language. As I wrote this book, it was with the expectation that this is your first time programming or you are not an experienced programmer.

How This Book Is Organized

We have broken the book into three parts, focusing each part on beginning concepts, intermediate, and advanced.

Conventions Used In This Book

Throughout the book, we have used a box to enclose script examples.

```
print ("Hello World")
```

Using Code Examples and Fair Use Laws

This book was written to help you learn to develop applications and games with the Lua scripting language. In general, you may use the code in this book in your programs and documentation. You do not need to contact us for permission to reproduce a portion of the code. You don't need to ask permission to write an app that uses any of the example code.

I reserve all rights for selling or distributing the examples in any format provided in this book. If you're not sure if your use falls outside of the Fair Use laws, please feel free to contact me at: DrBurton@BurtonsMediaGroup.com.

How to Contact Us

Please address any comments or questions to sales@BurtonsMediaGroup.com.
Join our discord server at https://discord.gg/tKSWMGh9fU

Why I Chose to Indie-Publish

The decision to Indie-publish was reached after a great deal of consideration. While there were numerous publishers interested (both academic and technical), I decided to release this first edition without the use of traditional publishers. There are many reasons why I made this decision, even though it will most likely lead to fewer sells.

First among my concerns was the price of the final book. I am sick of seeing textbooks at $100+. I feel such pricing places an undue burden upon students and schools. While publishers have cut the price slightly with the advent of eBooks and eTextbooks, it hasn't been enough in my opinion. By indie-publishing, I am only at the mercy of Apple, Amazon, Google, and Kobo.

My second concern was how rapidly software environments change. I personally hate having to purchase a new book for each major revision of the

software. I have stacks of books that are now completely useless. I decided to publish this as an eTextbook, which allows me to update and provide it to you, the reader, more rapidly. I will provide the updates between editions to the eBook to everyone who purchases the eTextbook through my website:
http://www.BurtonsMediaGroup.com/books/book-update/

However, if you received a copy of this book, either through a torrent or a friend, please purchase your personal copy through my website. This will provide you with the most recent version of the textbook and encourage me to continue to keep it updated. While I am doing this to help my students, I have bills to pay, and my wife is amazingly creative at keeping my 'honey-do' list up-to-date. Help me to avoid that list by buying a legitimate copy of this book.

On the downside of indie publishing, I do NOT have a team of people to proof and double-check everything in this book. I am sure that typos were entered by gremlins during the night. To make things more challenging, I have dyslexia. I did hire a person to proof the final version of the book but having read many books that were published by major companies and found errors in their books, I am sure that errors remain in this one. Please let me know if you find a typo via email drburton@burtonsmediagroup.com.

Curriculum

Part I: Introduction and Setup
>History of Lua
>Installing Lua
>Hello World
>Comments
>Variables
>String Variables
>Mathematics and Math Library
>Functions
>Decisions
>Loops

Part II: Intermediate Lua
>Input/Output Library
>Tables
>Pairs & iPairs
>Closure
>OS Library
>Modules
>Recursion

Part III: Advanced Lua
>Objects
>Metatables and Metamethods
>Additional Resources

Part 1:
Introductory Concepts of Lua

Chapter 1: Introduction to Lua

Lua is a lightweight scripting language that is widely used for embedded systems scripting top applications and games. Over the subsequent chapters, we will cover the basics of programming and how to create your own games or applications using Lua. In this chapter, we will cover topics such as:

> ➢ What is Lua and why you should learn it

> ➢ Getting started with Lua

> ➢ Using Lua.org and installing Visual Studio Code

> ➢ Basic commands in Lua programming language

Why Learn Lua?

Lua is an easy-to-learn scripting language that is widely used to support many applications in gaming and the technology industry. It is used in many embedded systems, top applications, and games.

In addition to game development, Lua is used in various other applications such as Adobe Photoshop Lightroom, Wireshark, VLC media player, and more. It is also used as a scripting language for web applications and server-side programming, where its lightweight design and efficiency come in handy.

What is a 'lightweight' scripting language? A lightweight programming language is one that has a small footprint and low overhead, meaning it requires fewer computer resources, such as memory and processing power, to run.

Lua is considered lightweight for two reasons:

➢ The Lua interpreter is very small and requires minimal resources to run. This makes it easy to embed into other applications, such as games or other software, without adding significant overhead.
➢ Lua is designed to be highly modular, meaning that it can be customized and extended to meet the needs of specific applications. This allows developers to create programs that are tailored to the needs of their application.

The most popular place you will find Lua in use is in games or game engines such as Roblox, Solar 2D, LÖVE 2D, and Defold:

1. Roblox: Lua is the primary scripting language used in Roblox. The Lua programming language is used to program the behavior of objects, create user interfaces, and more.

2. Solar 2D, formerly known as Corona SDK, is a cross-platform game engine that uses Lua as its scripting language. Lua is used to create game mechanics, handle user input, and create user interfaces. Solar 2D provides a range of Lua modules and libraries that developers can use to create games, including physics

engines, audio and video libraries, and more. You can find a lot of tutorials and books by the author on Solar 2D on YouTube and BurtonsMediagroup.com.

3. LÖVE 2D is an open-source framework for 2D game development. I first fell in love with this framework when I discovered LOVR, which is built on the LÖVE 2D engine and allows you to create VR applications using Lua with the extension LUVR.

4. Defold is another game engine that uses Lua as its primary scripting language. Lua scripts in Defold are used to create game mechanics, manage game assets, and handle user input. Defold's Lua engine is optimized for performance and includes a range of features, such as live coding, debugging, and profiling tools that make it easier to create high-quality games.

One of the first places I experienced Lua was playing World of Warcraft, where Lua scripting quickly found its way into my heart as a powerful tool that made the game even more enjoyable.

The History of the Lua

The Lua (pronounced LOO-ah, meaning "moon" in Portuguese) scripting language's development began in 1993 by a group of researchers from the Pontifical Catholic University of Rio de Janeiro in Brazil led by Roberto Ierusalimschy, Waldemar Celes, and Luiz Henrique de Figueiredo. The team were members of the Computer Graphics Technology Group (Tecgraf). Prior to this time, Brazil has stringent limitations on the importation of computer hardware and software, creating an atmosphere where Tecgraf and their clients were limited both politically and economically on what they could use for their projects.

In response to this challenge, the Tecgraf team began developing a new language that would be highly modular, extensible, and easy to learn. They drew inspiration from several existing programming languages, including Scheme, Modula, and Smalltalk, and incorporated many innovative features of their own.

The Lua language quickly gained popularity among developers in Brazil and around the world. Today, Lua is widely used in a variety of applications, from game development to scientific computing to web programming, and has become an important part of the programming landscape. The original goal was to create a language that was simple, efficient, and flexible enough to be used in a variety of applications.

The name "Lua" means "moon" in Portuguese, and it reflects the creators' fascination with astronomy. The language was initially designed to be embedded into other programs, providing an easy way for developers to extend the functionality of their software. Lua continues to be maintained by the LabLua, a part of the Computer Science department at the Pontifical Catholic University of Rio de Janeiro.

Lua Versions

The most current version of Lua is 5.4.6 at the time of this writing. Updates are released on a semi-regular basis as the language continues to evolve.

LuaJIT, or the Lua Just-In-Time interpreter, can take Lua script and convert it into machine code that can be executed directly by the computer's processor. This process of converting Lua code to machine code is referred to as "compilation."

By using a JIT compiler like LuaJIT, Lua programs can run much faster than they would with just the standard interpreter alone. This is because the JIT compiler can optimize the code in real-time, based on how it's actually being used during runtime.

In simple terms, LuaJIT takes Lua code and makes it run faster by compiling it into machine code on the fly. This makes Lua programs run more efficiently and quickly, which can be especially beneficial for performance-intensive applications like games and scientific simulations.

Getting Started with Lua

You can try Lua on the internet at https://www.lua.org/demo.html. While I do not recommend this as a long-term solution, it will allow you to try Lua and use follow along with the majority of examples in this textbook.

To use Lua as a developer, you should use it as a part of an IDE (Integrated Development Environment). There are several popular IDEs that provide Lua support. For the purposes of simplicity, we will be using Visual Studio Code from Microsoft which is fast, lightweight, and works the same on Mac and Windows. Some of the most popular tools that use Lua have their own IDE that allows you to easily incorporate your Lua code into their applications.

To install Lua on your personal computer, download the Lua binaries (i.e. the Lua Interpreter) from https://luabinaries.sourceforge.net/download.html.

LuaBinaries 5.4.2 - Release 1

lua-5.4.2_Sources.tar.gz	Source Code and Makefiles
lua-5.4.2_Sources.zip	Source Code and Makefiles
lua-5.4.2_Win32_bin.zip	Windows x86 Executables
lua-5.4.2_Win32_dllw6_lib.zip	Windows x86 DLL and Includes (MingW-w64 6 Built)
lua-5.4.2_Win64_bin.zip	Windows x64 Executables
lua-5.4.2_Win64_dllw6_lib.zip	Windows x64 DLL and Includes (MingW-w64 6 Built)
lua-5.4.2_MacOS1011_bin.tar.gz	MacOS X Intel Executables
lua-5.4.2_MacOS1011_lib.tar.gz	MacOS X Intel Library and Includes

Extract the download for your operating system to a folder on your hard drive. I extracted Windows 64 (i.e. Windows 10 or Windows 11) to C:\Lua.

Rename the Lua54.exe to Lua.exe. This will simplify your life.

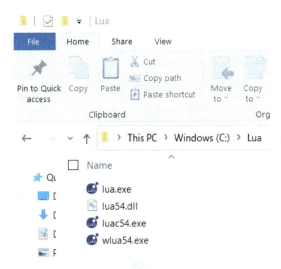

One more step to configure Lua for your development environment. In Windows, you will need to update the path to your Lua binary so that you can call the executable from a command line.

Open the System Environment Variables from your Settings.

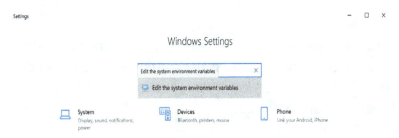

Click the "Environment Variables" at the bottom of the window.

In the "System variables" window, scroll down to "Path", then click the Edit button.

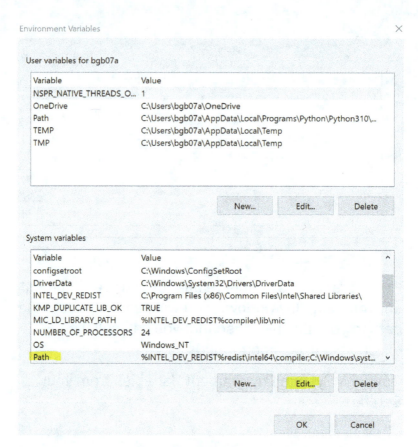

Click the New button. On the new line, type the path
to your Lua binaries. Just the path, you do not need
to include the name of the executable file. Click OK
when you are finished.

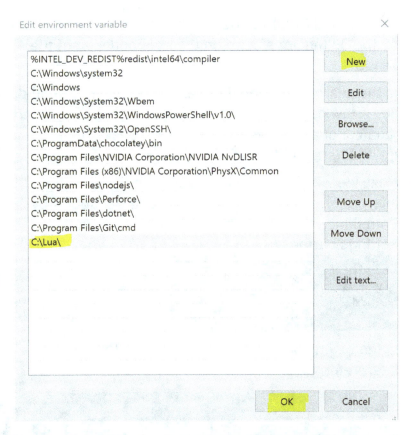

You have Lua ready to run on your system. Now we can install and configure Visual Studio Code.

You can download Visual Studio Code from https://code.visualstudio.com/download. It is available for Linux, Mac, and Windows.

Follow the standard installation process for your platform. When you launch Code, you will need to install the Lua extension.

Once Visual Studio Code is installed, open it and click on the "Extensions" icon on the left-hand side of the window.

In the search bar, type "Lua" and hit enter. You should see a few results. The one you want to install is called "Lua Language Server" by sumneko. Click on the green "Install" button to install it.

Next, we will install the connection to the Lua interpreter. Scroll down to "Local Lua Debugger" by Tom Blind. Click on "install." Finally, click on the Settings button

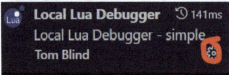

In the Extension Settings, type in the path to your Lua interpreter

Now we can begin scripting in Lua in Visual Studio Code!

Hello World in Lua

One of the basic commands in Lua programming language is the 'print' command. You can use the print command to output simple information. For example, to output "Hello World" in Lua, you can use the following command:

```
print("Hello World")
```

Save the file as "hello.lua".

To see the program run, you will need a terminal window. Click on the three dots beside Run in the menu bar at the top of the window and select Terminal > New Terminal.

This will open a terminal window at the bottom of your screen. Tap the F5 key or click the Run > Start Debugging in the menu bar.

You should see "Hello World" displayed in the terminal window.

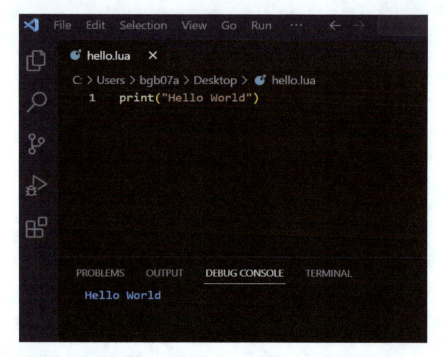

This is making use of the Local Lua Debugger that we installed through the extensions. Visual Studio Code is now able to execute any Lua program and display the results in the Debug Console or Output.

You can also run the program from the terminal window. Click on "Terminal" in the terminal window. Navigate to the folder where you saved hello.lua. In my case, I saved it on my desktop.

Type **lua hello.lua** and you should see the same results as pressing F5.

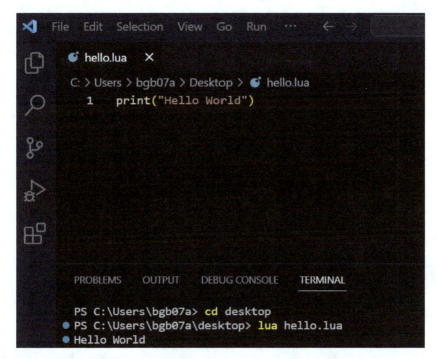

By including the path to the Lua folder where we save the binary files, we can call the lua executable from any command line on our system.

Troubleshooting in Lua

In Lua, the **print** statement is primarily used to output information to the console or terminal. This allows developers to quickly see the current value of variables, where they are at in the program, and to perform basic troubleshooting. Print is one of the most useful tools for being able to troubleshoot quickly and easily in Lua.

In more complex programs, it can be helpful to see what line or file you're currently working on. Using the print command, you can easily enter what line and file you're working on. This makes troubleshooting much easier, especially in large programs. Adding a comma between information in the print adds a tab break between the two parts, making it easier to read and get the information on the screen quickly and easily.

Another useful tool for troubleshooting in Lua is the ability to concatenate strings using two periods ("**..**") . Concatenation is the process of joining two strings together. For example, you can join the two strings "hello" and "world" together by typing "print('hello'..'world')". Note that concatenation joins the two strings as they are, it does not add any spaces.

Documenting Your Program

Commenting your code is critical in programming, especially if you ever hope to do maintenance, troubleshooting, or work on it the next day. In Lua, comments can be added by typing two dashes or minus signs.

```
-- It is a good idea to comment your code
```

Anything after the minus signs will be treated as a comment and not evaluated by the interpreter; it ignores everything in a comment.

Inline comments can also be added by placing two dashes at the end of a line.

```
print ("Hello world!") -- Everything after the dashes is a comment
```

Block comments can be added by typing two dashes followed by two bracket characters. The block comment is ended with two right brackets.

```
C: > Users > bgb07a > Desktop >  hello.lua
1    print("Hello".."World")
2    -- this is a comment
3
4    --[[ This is a block
5    comment and it can span multiple lines]]
```

```
PROBLEMS    OUTPUT    DEBUG CONSOLE    TERMINAL
    HelloWorld
```

Conclusion

Lua is a very powerful scripting language that is easy to learn and widely used throughout the industry. In this chapter, we covered the basics of Lua programming language, including what it is, why you should learn it, how to get started, and basic commands. With this knowledge, you can start developing your own games or applications using Lua.

Questions

1. What is the primary purpose of the print command in Lua?

2. What is Lua and why is it widely used?

3. What are the topics covered in the chapter about Lua programming language?

4. What is the meaning of the term 'lightweight' scripting language?

5. What are the reasons why Lua is considered a lightweight scripting language?

6. What are some of the applications that use Lua besides gaming?

7. What are some of the popular game engines that use Lua?

8. Who developed the Lua programming language and why?

9. What is the current version of Lua and how often are updates released?

10. What is LuaJIT and how does it optimize Lua programs?

Going Deeper

You can learn more about the history of Lua at lua.org

Dr. Burton's videos introducing Lua:
Introduction to the Lua Scripting Language -
https://youtu.be/-iU1pCgmjx4
Using Print and comments in Lua -
https://youtu.be/7sj-qf99RPk

Chapter 2: Variables

Variables are a critical component of all programming languages. In this chapter, we will learn about the eight different types of variables available in the Lua scripting language.

Learning Objectives

In this chapter, we will learn about Lua's variable types. By the end of this chapter, you should be able to:

> Know the difference between local and global variables.

> Understand the default variable types in Lua.

> Explain how to use the "type" command in Lua.

Naming Variables

When we use a variable, we are creating an object. Just as in the real world, an object can be anything. And, of course, we need a name for the object. Whenever we assign an object to a variable, we are essentially giving that object a name. Everything that the object is will be stored and referred to through that assigned name. Just as you are called by a name, so are the objects within Lua. Using this name, we can use the object later in the app.

It is critical that each object has a unique name. Imagine a teacher asking Pat to answer a question in a class. But everyone in the class is named Pat. We have the same problem if we reuse the same variable names. Make your objects feel special; give each one a unique name.

There are a few rules to the naming of variables:

> A variable can be any combination of letters, numbers, or underscores

> A variable must not begin with a number

> A variable cannot contain a space or any symbol except an underscore

> Variables are case-sensitive. myVariable is not the same as MyVariable

Valid	Invalid
Variable1	1Variable
My_Variable	My Variable
_variable	-variable
variable12345	variable12.345

Local vs. Global Variables

Most of us have the experience, at one point or another, where we are given a 'temporary' name. Perhaps during school, there were two students with the same first name in a class, so they would have their last initial also used: thus two Heathers became HeatherA and HeatherB. Or maybe you were given a nickname in school or athletics. Usually, these different names were short-lived or only used in limited situations.

In programming, we have two types of variables: local and global. As we progress through the rest of this book (and any other programming language that you learn) think of the differences this way: a local variable is a short-lived name given to an object, much like that short-lived nickname in school. A global variable is a long-lasting name and can be used throughout a program, anywhere in a program.

How do you tell them apart? Easy. A local variable will always have the keyword **local** in front of it the first time it is used in an app. A global variable will never have, or be initialized with the word local. Many Lua developers place an underscore in front of global variables so that they can be easily identified.

Declaring a local variable:

```
local textObject
local myNewPicture
local backgroundImage
```

Declaring a global variable:

```
textObject
_myNewPicture
backgroundImage
```

The preference in programming is to always use local

variables whenever possible. Local variables use less memory and will help you avoid naming problems in more complex programs.

Variable Types in Lua

In Lua, we have eight default variable types: nil, number, string, boolean, table, function, userdata, and thread. It should be noted that Lua is a dynamically typed language, meaning you don't have to explicitly declare a variable type when creating your variables. You just simply declare your variable, and the Just-In-Time Compiler (LuaJIT) will automatically type the variable to what it thinks is the correct variable type.

Below are the basic variable types and the information that they can store.

The Nil Variable Type

Nil is the default variable type in Lua. All variables when they are created are, by default, nil until they are given a value. Nil is also used to clear variables or make them available for garbage collection to free up memory. If you are done using a variable inside a programming project, you can set it to nil to remove it from memory.

Examples of nil variables:

```
local myVariable = nil
local newVariable
```

The Number Data Type

The number data type is used to store all numeric values. It is a double-precision floating-point real number for storage that includes for all types, including what we would normally consider an integer or other data precision types for numeric values. Internally, Lua stores all numeric values as a 64-bit double-precision floating-point number.

Examples of numeric variables:

```
local myInteger = 1
local myDecimal = 3.214
local anotherInteger = 0
```

Numeric Operators

Lua provides all of the standard operators for working with mathematical equations that you will find in other programming languages:

Addition operator +
    print (2 + 2)

Subtraction operator -
    print (10 - 5)

Division operator /
    print (8 / 2)

Multiplication operator *
    print (5*3)

Exponent operator (the power of) ^

```
print (5^2)
```

Lua calculates values from left to right. When working with mathematical equations, you can enforce values to be calculated first by wrapping them in parentheses. When Lua finds a mathematical equation, it always calculates the innermost equation contained within parentheses first, then works its way to the outer nested equations. For example

```
print (2 + 2 * 2 + 2)
-- will return a different result than
print ((2 + 2) * (2 + 2))

print (3 + 3 * 3 * 3 + 3)
-- will return a different result than
print ((3 + 3 * 3) * (3 + 3))
-- will return a different result than
print (((3 + 3) * 3) * (3 + 3))
```

Dividing by Zero

In Lua, all mathematical expressions return a numeric value, with the exception of equations where a number is divided by zero. For instance, take the following expression:

```
print ( 5 / 0 )
```

In many languages, this expression would raise an error. However, in Lua, this expression would print the value 'Inf', meaning infinite. 'Inf' is not usable in a numeric equation and thus should be caught where possible in a value check. This should preferably be carried out before the equation by checking if the divisor value is zero. A quick way that you can check the result of the equation is to use the following code:

```
result = 5/0
print ( result == 1/0 )
-- outputs true
```

Lua provides quite an extensive number of math functions. We'll be looking at these in Chapter 4.

The String Data Type

The string data type is a more complex variable type that stores a sequence of characters. You can create a string using either single or double quotes, or you can create a multi-line string using double-square brackets [[ ]]. Strings have their own styles as well as escape characters that are available to us through Lua. We will explore the string data type further in the next chapter.

Examples of string variables:

```
local myString1 = 'Hello world'
local anotherString = "Hello world with double quote"
local myString2 = [[You can have multiple
lines of text when you
use square brackets. ]]
```

The Boolean Data Type

The Boolean data type is used to store both true and false values. Booleans work a little bit differently in the Lua language. We are not limited to just true or false values to represent or output the meaning of a boolean. Nil would also return a false.

Examples of boolean variables:

```
local aTrueBoolean = true
local aFalseBoolean = false
```

Tables in Lua

Tables are a powerful and useful tool inside of the Lua scripting language. They store the data as an associative array, meaning that it can store strings next to integers next to reals next to booleans. It doesn't make any difference, and they can be indexed by any other variable type inside the system. To create an array, you use the curly brackets to delineate it. We will discuss tables in more detail in Chapter 9.

Examples of tables:

```
local myTable = { } --an empty table
local myTable = { 'First Item', 2, 'Third item' }
```

Userdata

Lua provides the userdata variable type that allows us to create custom data types using the C programming language. Userdata acts as a bridge between Lua and C, enabling us to integrate C libraries and functionalities seamlessly into our Lua programs.

For example, we could create a data type for a vector (a mathematical or geometrical representation that includes magnitude and direction). In Lua, we can define a userdata type and name it Vector:

```
userdata Vector
```

We can then create an instance of the vector using newuserdata.

```
local v = newuserdata(Vector)
```

You can then work with the fields of the vector variable using dot notation, which will be discussed further in later chapters.

```
v.x = 10
print(v.x)

Output
10
```

Threads

Threads in Lua allow us to perform concurrent programming, enabling multiple tasks to run simultaneously. Threads are lightweight and have their own separate execution contexts, making them suitable for scenarios where parallel execution is required.

To create a thread in Lua, we use the thread.create() function. It takes a function as an argument, which will be executed in the new thread.

```
local t = thread.create(function()
   -- Thread code goes here
end)
```

To start a thread, we use the thread.start() function. It takes the thread handle as an argument and begins the execution of the associated function.

```
thread.start(t)
```

Joining threads allows us to wait for a thread's execution to complete before proceeding further in our program. To join a thread, we use the thread.join() function.

```
thread.join(t)
```

Threads can communicate with each other by passing messages. Lua provides a mechanism called channels for inter-thread communication. Channels act as communication queues, allowing threads to send and receive data.

Using the "Type" Command

If you want to check on what type a variable is, you can use the "type" command.

For example, if you declare a variable called "myVariable" and set it equal to nil, using the command "print(type(myVariable))" will output "nil" since it has not been initially declared for any other variable type.

Examples of using the type command:

```
local myInteger = 1
local myDecimal = 3.214
local myString1 = 'Hello world'
print( type( myInteger ) )
print( type( myDecimal ) )
print( type( myString1 ) )

output:
number
number
string
```

Conclusion

In this chapter, we explored the different variable types in Lua, including nil, number, string, boolean, and table. We also learned how to use the "type" command and how tables can be indexed.

Questions

1. What are the eight default variable types built into Lua?

2. How does Lua handle variable typing?

3. What is the default variable type in Lua?

4. How can you clear a variable or make it available for garbage collection in Lua?

5. How do you check the type of a variable in Lua?

6. How does Lua store numeric values internally?

7. How can you create a multi-line string in Lua?

8. What is the boolean variable type used for in Lua?

9. What does a false condition in Lua mean when using boolean values?

10. What is the table variable type used for in Lua?

Going Deeper

Dr. Burton's tutorial on variable types -
https://youtu.be/2qGxUgC-Tmo

Lua.org variable types - https://www.lua.org/pil/2.html

Chapter 3: Working with Strings in Lua

In this chapter, we will explore the power and versatility of working with strings in the Lua scripting language. We will learn how to manipulate strings using various operators and tools in Lua.

Learning outcomes

➢ Understand how to create a string variable

➢ Understand the length operator and its usefulness in Lua

➢ Understand how to concatenate strings

➢ Understand the use of the tostring command in converting numbers to strings

➢ Understand the use of escape sequences in Lua

➢ Become familiar with the string library commands and their usage

Quotation Marks

There are three types of quotation marks you can use to contain strings. The Lua interpreter requires that the quotation marks be **dumb quotes** (i.e., NOT smart quotes). Most editors such as Visual Studio Code use dumb quotes by default.

What are dumb quotes? A dumb quotation mark is a mark that is straight (" "), whereas a smart quote curls to the right or left depending on if the mark is beginning the quote or ending the quote (" ").

These are single quotes:

'This is a string'

double quotes:

"This is also a string"

or even double square brackets used to denote a string.

[[This is a square bracketed string]]

Square brackets represent literal strings. While in single or double quoted strings, the compiler will look for special characters, such as escape sequences or control characters (we will explore these next), everything contained within square brackets is treated exactly as given. Thus, if a tab is used within the string, it will be treated by the compiler as a literal tab and will be visible when output to the user.

Square brackets are useful for working with strings that span more than one line. If you try to include line feeds in a single or double quoted strings, you will generate an error:

[[This is
a string that
spans multiple
lines]]

"This string

> will raise an
> error"

It is possible, however, to enforce multiple line traversal with single or double quoted strings by using an escape character at the end of each line:

> "This string \
> will no longer \
> raise an error"

Escape Sequences

In Lua, escape sequences are special codes we use to tell the computer to do something special when we write text. Imagine you are writing a secret message to your friend, and you want to add some cool effects. For example, if you want to jump to the next line, you can use the escape sequence "\n" at the end of your sentence. It's like pressing the "Enter" key on your keyboard.

When you write text in a computer program, you have different types of quotes you can use. But sometimes, you want to use the same kind of quote inside your text, and that's when escape sequences come to the rescue!

If you want to use a quote of the same kind inside your text, you need to add a special backslash (\) before it. It's like telling the computer, "Hey, this quote is not the end of the text; it's just a regular quote!"

For example, you can write:

"This is 'fine for quoting' with single quotes."
and not have any problems.

But if you want to use the same quote inside double
quotes, you need to do this:
"This \"needs escaping\" to not cause an error"

to output:
This "needs escaping" to not cause an error.

You can also use special codes to create cool effects.
For example, you can use "\t" to make an indentation
or tab, "\v" to add space above a line, and "\n" to start
a new line. And if you want to use a backslash in your
text, you need to write two backslashes: "Only one of
these \ will be visible."

Indentation/tab:
    "\tThis string starts off indented"

vertical tabs (\v):
    "\vThis string will have padding above it"

newline characters (\n):
    "This string\nwill appear on two lines"

and including a backslash:

    "Only one of these \\ will be visible"

Concatenating Strings

Concatenation is the joining of two separate strings
into a single string. Concatenation is done using the

concatenation character '..' or two periods in a row, without any spacing between them. When concatenating strings, the original strings remain unchanged. For example:

```
strOne = "abc"
strTwo = "def"
strThree = strOne .. strTwo
print (strOne)

Output
abc

print (strTwo)

Output
def

print (strThree)

Output:
abcdef
```

If you would like a space to appear between the two strings, then add it to one of the strings, or add it separately when concatenating:

```
strThree = strOne .. ' ' .. strTwo
print (strThree)

Output:
abc def
```

The Length Operator

One of the useful tools in working with Lua is the pound (or hashtag #) length operator. The length operator returns the length of an object. For instance, if you have a string variable, you can use the length operator to determine the number of characters in that string.

Example:

```
local my_string = "Hello, world!"
local length = #my_string
print(length)
```

Output:
13

In the example above, the length operator returns the length of the variable my_string, which is 13 characters.

Concatenation

Another commonly used operator inside of the Lua scripting language is the concatenation operator. Concatenation is the joining of two strings together. In Lua, we can use the .. (two periods) operator to concatenate two strings. The concatenation operator does NOT add spaces or other punctuation; you will have to add that yourself.

```
local greeting = "Hello"
local name = "John"
local message = greeting .. " " .. name .. "!"

print(message)
```

Output:
```
Hello John!
```

In the example above, the greeting and name variables are concatenated using the .. operator, and the resulting string is stored in a variable named message.

tostring Command

Frequently, when we are working with variables, we may not be sure if a number that is being stored in a variable is a string or an actual numeric value. In Lua, we can use the tostring command to convert any numeric value to a string.

```
local number = 42
local string_number = tostring( number )
print( string_number )
print( type( number ) )
print( type( string_number ) )
```

Output:
```
42
```

```
numeric
string
```

In the example above, the tostring command converts the numeric value of number to a string, which is stored in the string_number variable. We used the **type** command to determine the variable type.

Assigning Multiple Variables

The Lua scripting language allows us to assign multiple variables in one line. The values are assigned in sequence, with the first value assigned to the first variable, the second value assigned to the second variable, and so on. If you mistakenly leave out a value for a variable, it will receive the nil value.

```
local a, b, c = "hi", "hello"
print(a, b, c)
```

Output
```
hi  hello   nil
```

In the example above, the variables a and b are assigned values "hi" and "hello", respectively. Since no value is assigned to c, it receives the nil value.

String Library

Let's explore the string library. The string library consists of a series of commands that simplify and enhance string manipulation in your programs. We will cover the usage of each command to help you effectively work with strings. Commands that use the string library include the keyword 'string' followed by a period then the specific command. The string should be lowercase when used as part of a command.

Commonly used string commands:

string.len(s)	Returns the length of a string (s)
string.find(s, a)	Returns the location of string a in string s
string.upper(s)	Converts the entire string (s) to uppercase
string.lower(s)	Converts the entire string (s) to lowercase
string.sub(s, x, y)	Extracts a part of the string (s) from the xth character to the yth character.
string.gsub(s, a, r)	Replaces all occurrences of a with r in string s
string.match(s, p)	Returns a string that matches the given pattern p
string.byte(s)	Converts a string (s) to it's ASCII value.

string.char(n)	Converts an ASCII value (n) to a string

Strings in Lua are immutable. This means that when you apply a string library command to a string, it does not change the original string. Instead, it creates a new string.

string.len

Like the pound or hashtag symbols (#) that we used earlier in the chapter, the string.len command returns the length of a string.

```
local my_string = "Hello, world!"
print( string.len(my_string))
```
Output:
```
13
```

string.find

Occasionally, you need to know where a particular string of characters exists within a given larger string. For instance, you might like to locate potential phone numbers, dates, or offensive words. You can perform this process by using the 'find' function:

```
local str = "The quick brown fox jumped over the
lazy dog"
print ( string.find(str, "brown") )
```

```
Output:
11       15
```

The result of the function is the location of the starting character for the match as well as the location of the ending character. In this case 'brown' begins at character 11 and ends at character 15.

The 'find' function returns the first match only, so further matches will need to be requested using a starting location beyond a previous match.

For example, our previous match ended at character 15. Therefore, we could repeat the search for the word 'brown' from character 16 onwards. We do this by providing a third parameter; the search start location.

```
print ( string.find(str, "brown", 16) )

Output
nil
```

This time, no result was found as the search word did not reoccur in the string that was searched. Thus, the function returned 'nil'.

string.upper and string.lower

In the previous examples, you saw how to search for and extract characters in a string, but what would happen if you were to run the following example?

```
local str = "The quick brown fox jumped over the
lazy dog"
print ( string.find( str, 't' ) )
```

One would assume the result printed to screen would be the number 1, matching the 't' from the word 'The'. If you guessed this, you'd be incorrect. Instead, the output will be 33, matching the 't' from the second occurrence of the word 'the'. This is because the lowercase letter 't' and the uppercase letter 'T' are considered different characters and are therefore not the same.

When performing a search where you are not concerned about the case of the letter or word you wish to find, it is easiest to convert the string to consist of all lower or upper case letters first. This is performed using the 'lower' and 'upper' functions, respectively. For example

```
local str = "The quick brown fox jumped over the
lazy dog"
print ( string.lower(str) )
Output:
the quick brown fox jumped over the lazy dog

print ( string.upper(str) )
Output:
THE QUICK BROWN FOX JUMPED OVER THE LAZY
DOG
```

string.sub

Occasionally, you might want to extract a segment of a string as a new string. For example, we may want to copy the chunk of characters starting from the beginning of the string and ending with the word 'brown' to a new string. We could use string.find to learn that the word 'brown' ends at character 15, but to extract the text before and including that location, we use the 'sub' function. The 'sub' is short for sub-string.:

```
local str = "The quick brown fox jumped over the
lazy dog"
print ( string.sub(str, 0, 15) )
```

Output
The quick brown

string.gsub

Global substitution replaces all occurrences of a given pattern in a string. In Lua, we perform global substitution using the 'gsub' function.

For example, we might like to replace the letter 'o' in a sentence with another character:

```
local str = "The quick brown fox jumped over the lazy
dog"
print ( string.gsub( str, "o", "@" ) )
```

Note the number 4 at the end of the output. This is not a typo. Lua returns the number of replaced instances of the pattern within the string as well as the resulting string itself. Being able to return more than one value from a function is a powerful feature of Lua that we'll examine in greater detail in a later chapter.

Global substitution can also be used to replace whole words or sentences. You can specify a special pattern string that works similarly to regular expressions in other languages, though not quite so powerful. For example, if we wanted to replace any five-letter words beginning with the letter b with the word "red", we could use the following code:

```
print ( string.gsub( str, "b....", "red" ) )
```

Output
The quick red fox jumped over the lazy dog

The period symbol when used in a pattern, represents a wildcard character, so will match any character in the string. In the previous example, we simply said "replace any five characters that begin with the letter 'b' with the word 'red'". The wildcard character will also match spaces in your strings.

string.match

As well as finding the location of a string of characters in a string, Lua will also find which words in a string match a given pattern. You perform this task using the 'match' function. The parameters for 'match' are the same as with 'find'. However, rather than returning the location, 'match' returns the actual word found. For example:

```
local str = "The quick brown fox jumped over the
lazy dog"
print ( string.match(str, "b....") )
Output
brown
```

As with 'find', match also accepts the starting location as its third parameter.

When using match, you will use a pattern as the search criteria, because you already know which word will match when using non-pattern based searches.

string.byte

You can find the ASCII value (American Standard Code for Information Interchange) of any character in your string by using the string.byte function. For example, to get the ASCII value of the fifth character, you would use:

```
local str = "The quick brown fox jumped over the lazy
dog"
```

```
print ( string.byte(str, 5) )
Output:
113
```

ASCII characters are useful when you want to check for a character's actual value as opposed to its visual representative value. For instance, you may want to check that a character is the letter 'o' rather than a '0' (zero), or you may want to compare accented and non-accented letters.

string.char

Lua also provides the means to get string characters from ASCII values, using the 'char' function:

```
print ( string.char(113) )
Output:
q
```

The 'char' function can take multiple parameters, so it's possible to return a whole string from a number of ASCII codes:

```
print ( string.char(65, 66, 67) )

Output
ABC
```

Conclusion

In conclusion, this chapter has covered essential concepts related to working with strings in Lua. Quotation marks, escape sequences, string concatenation, the length operator, and the string library commands are fundamental tools that every programmer should be familiar with.

Understanding the different types of quotation marks and their proper usage is crucial for correctly representing strings in Lua. Additionally, knowing how to handle escape sequences enables us to include special characters and match quotes within strings effectively.

Concatenating strings allows us to combine multiple strings into a single entity, enabling flexible and dynamic string manipulation. The length operator helps us determine the size of a string, which is often necessary for various programmatic operations.

Lastly, the string library provides an extensive range of functions that facilitate string manipulation tasks. These functions allow us to search for substrings, convert case, extract specific portions of a string, replace patterns, perform word matching, and manipulate ASCII values.

By mastering these concepts, programmers gain the ability to manipulate and work with strings efficiently, a skill that is invaluable in many programming scenarios. Strings play a vital role in storing and manipulating textual data, making it crucial to have a solid understanding of the concepts presented in this chapter.

Questions

1) What is the pound or len operator in Lua, and how is it used?

2) What is concatenation, and how is it used to join two strings together in Lua?

3) What is the tostring function, and how is it useful in Lua programming?

4) How can you create a multi-line string in Lua?

5) What is the syntax for assigning multiple variables in a single line of code in Lua?

6) What is the purpose of escape sequences in strings?

7) How can you convert a numeric value to a string in Lua?

8) How can you assign multiple variables in a single line in Lua?

9) What is the purpose of the string library in Lua, and what are some commonly used commands?

10) How can you replace all occurrences of a specific pattern within a string in Lua?

Exercises

1) Write a Lua program that assigns a sentence to a variable and then prints the length of that sentence using the string.len function.

2) Create a Lua program that assigns a string to a variable and replaces all occurrences of the letter 'a' with the symbol '@' using the string.gsub function.

3) Write a Lua program that assigns a sentence to a variable and then checks if the sentence contains the word "Lua" using the string.find function. Display a message indicating whether the word was found or not.

4) Develop a Lua program that assigns a sentence to a variable and converts all the characters to uppercase using the string.upper function. Print the modified sentence.

5) Create a Lua program that assigns a sentence to a variable and checks if it starts with the letter 'T' using the string.sub function.

Going Deeper

Additional resources on using the string Library in Lua:
https://www.lua.org/manual/5.4/manual.html#6.4

Chapter 4: Math and the Math Library

In this chapter, we'll dive into the exciting world of Lua math operations and explore the powerful math library. Lua is capable of performing various mathematical calculations. We will also discover the "to number" function, a handy tool for converting strings into numbers effortlessly. So, let's roll up our sleeves and get ready to crunch some numbers!

Learning Outcomes

In this chapter, we will learn about the mathematical functions and math library available in the Lua Scripting language. Specifically, we will:

1) Understand how Lua stores numbers in variables

2) Master the order of operations in Lua math

3) Apply the modulus operator in Lua

4) Explore Lua's math library

The Number Variable Type

Lua, like many programming languages, stores numbers in variables for processing and manipulation. Understanding how Lua handles numbers internally can help us write efficient and accurate code.

In Lua, numbers can be stored as either integers or real (floating point). Integers are whole numbers without any fractional part, while real are numbers that can have a decimal component. Lua automatically chooses the appropriate representation based on the assigned value. Lua uses 64-bit integers and double-precision (64-bit) floats, providing a level of accuracy that will handle most applications.

Math Order of Operations in Lua

Just like in most programming languages, Lua provides a set of basic mathematical operators. These include exponential, multiplication, division, modulus (or modulo), addition, and subtraction. Understanding the order of precedence for these operators is crucial for performing accurate calculations.

Here's a quick rundown of the order of precedence from highest to lowest in Lua:

 ➢ Exponential - ^
 ➢ Unary (negative numbers)
 ➢ Multiplication, division, and modulus - *, /, %
 ➢ Addition and subtraction - +, -

```
-- Perform the calculation (5 + 3) * 2
local result = ( 5 + 3 ) * 2
print( result )

Output
16
```

Remember, parentheses are your friends! Just as you learned in math class in school, calculations within parentheses are completed before calculations outside of a set of parentheses. Using parentheses ensures that calculations are performed in the desired order. Don't hesitate to use them liberally to avoid any confusion.

Modulus: The Remainder Calculation

Lua provides the modulus operator (%), which calculates the remainder of a division operation. This can be particularly useful in game development or when dealing with moving objects on a screen. For instance, when we compute the modulus of 5 divided by 4, we obtain a remainder of 1.

-- Calculate the result of 27 divided by 4 and find the remainder

```
local quotient = 27 / 4
print("Quotient: " .. quotient)
```
Output
6.75

```
local remainder = 27 % 4
print("Remainder: " .. remainder)
```
Output
3

---

tonumber

Like the tostring command covered in the previous chapter, Lua provides a command to convert numbers that are stored as strings back to numerical values. If the string contains non-numeric characters, the result will be nil.

```
local test = "42"
print( tonumber( test ))

Output
42

local test = "a42"
print( tonumber( test ))

Output
nil
```

Exploring the Math Library

Lua comes with a range of built-in libraries that expand its capabilities. One such library is the math library, which allows us to perform advanced computations quickly and efficiently.

The math library is extensive. Here is a full list of the available functions in the math library. Each starts with the keyword math. In all examples x and y are a number:

➢ math.abs(x) – returns the absolute value of x.

- math.acos(x) – returns the arc cosine of x in radians (a number between 0 and pi). x must be between -1 and 1.
- math.asin(x) - returns the arc sine of x in radians (a number between –pi/2 and pi/2). x must be between -1 and 1.
- math.atan(x) - returns the arc tangent of x in radians (a number between –pi/2 and pi/2).
- math.atan2(y, x) - returns the arc tangent of y/x (in radians). Useful when converting rectangular coordinates to polar coordinates.
- math.ceil(x) – returns the smallest integer larger than or equal to x.
- math.cos(x) – returns the cosine of x in the range of -1 to 1.
- math.cosh(x) – returns the hyperbolic cosine of x.
- math.deg(x) – converts a radian value (x) to degrees.
- math.exp(x) – returns the value of e^x.
- math.floor(x) – returns the largest integer smaller than or equal to x.
- math.fmod(x, y) – returns the remainder of dividing x by y, rounding the quotient towards zero.
- math.frexp(x) – returns the split of x into a normalized fraction and an exponent.
- math.huge - returns a value larger than or equal to any other numerical value (basically

an infinite number, but computers don't handle infinite very well, so a really, really big number).

➢ math.inf - same as math.huge, returns a value larger than or equal to any other numerical value.

➢ math.ldexp(m, e) – returns m* 2^e.

➢ math.log(x) – returns the natural logarithm of x.

➢ math.log10(x) – returns the base-10 logarithm of x.

➢ math.max(x, ...) – returns the largest value from the supplied arguments.

➢ math.min(x, ...) – returns the smallest value from the supplied arguments.

➢ math.modf(x) – returns the integer part of x and the fractional part of x.

➢ math.pi – returns pi.

➢ math.pow(x, y) – returns x^y.

➢ math.rad(x) – converts radians to an angle in degrees.

➢ math.random([x][, y]) – returns a pseudo-random number. If x is not provided, then a number between 0 and 1 is generated. If x is provided, then a number between 1 and x. If x and y are provided, then a number between x and y is generated.

➢ math.randomseed(x) – sets x as the seed number for the pseudo-random number generator. If the same x is always used, the sequence of random numbers will be the same.

➢ math.round(x) – returns the x rounded to the nearest integer.
➢ math.sin(x) - returns the sine of x in the range of -1 to 1.
➢ math.sinh(x) - returns the hyperbolic sine of x.
➢ math.sqrt(x) – returns the square root of x.
➢ math.tan(x) - returns the tangent of x.
➢ math.tanh(x) – returns the hyperbolic tangent of x.

Examples of the math library in action:

```
-- Example 1: Using the value of pi from the math
library
local radius = 5
local circumference = 2 * math.pi * radius
print(circumference)
```

Output
31.415926535897

The Random Function

Game developers rejoice! The math library's random function is a valuable tool for generating random numbers. Without providing any parameters, math.random will produce a random number between 0 and 1. However, if you desire a random number within a specific range, say between 1 and 10, Lua has got you covered!

While using the random number generator, it's important to note that it operates as a pseudo-random generator. This means that without reseeding the random number generator via math.randomseed, the sequence of random numbers generated will remain the same each time the program runs. If you want different sequences, you can easily achieve that by using the random seed function. For instance, you can use the operating system library to get the current time and base the random number generation on it.

```
-- Generating a random number between 1 and 100
math.randomseed( os.time() )
local randomNumber = math.random(1, 100)
print(randomNumber)
```

Output
46 – Random number (your results will be different)

Trigonometry in Lua

For those venturing into the world of trigonometry, Lua's math library has your back! You can effortlessly compute sine, cosine, tangent, and other trigonometric functions by invoking the corresponding functions from the math library. These functions can come in handy when tackling geometry or physics problems.

```
-- Example: Calculate the sine of 45 degrees
local angleInDegrees = 45
local angleInRadians = math.rad( angleInDegrees )
local sineValue = math.sin( angleInRadians )
print( sineValue )
```

Output
0.70710678118655

Conclusion

In this chapter, we delved into the fascinating world of Lua programming and explored various concepts related to math operations and the math library. We learned how Lua internally stores numbers as integers or doubles, and how the tonumber function can be used to automatically convert strings into numbers. We also discussed the basic operators available in Lua, such as exponential, multiplication, division, modulus, addition, and subtraction, and their order of precedence.

To ensure accurate calculations, we emphasized the importance of using parentheses when necessary and how they can affect the order of operations. We also discovered the usefulness of the modulus operator, particularly in game development scenarios, where it can help calculate remainders and facilitate object movement on the screen.

Furthermore, we explored Lua's built-in math library, which offers a wealth of advanced computational capabilities. We focused on two commonly used functions: pi, which provides the value of π for calculations requiring it, and random, which generates random numbers within specified ranges. We also touched on the notion of reseeding the random number generator to achieve different sequences of random numbers, or leveraging the operating system library to use the current time as a parameter.

Lastly, we briefly mentioned Lua's support for trigonometric functions in the math library, allowing us to compute sine, cosine, tangent, and more.

Questions

1) How does Lua store numbers in variables?

2) What are the two types of numbers that Lua can store?

3) How does Lua determine the appropriate representation for a number?

4) What is the order of precedence for mathematical operations in Lua?

5) What is the modulus operator in Lua, and what is its purpose?

6) What does the tonumber command in Lua do?

7) What value does the tonumber command return if the string contains non-numeric characters?

8) What are some examples of functions available in Lua's math library?

9) How does Lua's random function work, and what can it be used for?

10) How can you generate a random number within a specific range using Lua's random function?

Exercises

1) Calculate the result of (5 + 3) * 2 using Lua.

2) Write a Lua program to find the remainder when 45 is divided by 4.

3) Use Lua's math library to calculate the value of sine(45 degrees).

4) Generate a random number between 1 and 100 using Lua's math library.

5) Write a Lua program that converts a temperature in Celsius to Fahrenheit using the formula: Fahrenheit = Celsius * (9/5) + 32.

Going Deeper

A complete list of Lua's math library - https://www.lua.org/manual/5.4/manual.html#6.7

Chapter 5: Functions in Lua

In this chapter, we will explore the usage and creation of functions in the Lua scripting language. Functions are essential tools that allow us to organize and reuse segments of code. By creating functions, we can perform specific computations and calculations whenever needed. Let's dive into the basics of functions and how they can be used effectively in Lua.

Learning Outcomes

> Understand the concept of functions and their importance in organizing code.

> Differentiate between function declaration methods in Lua.

> Comprehend the usage of parameters in functions.

> Return values from functions to provide results to the calling code.

> Handle multiple return values from functions and store them in variables.

> Grasp the concept of variable scope and understand the difference between local and global variables.

Functions

A function is a small segment of a program that we might need to use one or more times in our program.

Say you have created an app that has a button on the screen. In this app, every time the button is tapped, the button is moved to a new location. Now, we don't want this app just randomly moving the button, nor do we want it continuously moving the button. We only want the button to move after it has been tapped. This can be managed by creating a function.

A function begins with the keyword 'function' (surprised?) followed by the name of the function and any parameters to be passed. A function always ends with the keyword 'end'. In between these two keywords will be the commands and operations that you want to be executed when the function is called.

Always use an original name for your function (just like your variables) that describes what the function accomplishes. It is a common mistake to name a function the same as a variable name that you are using. It is bad programming practice and will create confusion as you begin to create more complex programs. Think of it like this: how confusing is it in a classroom when you have 5 people named Ashley or Jacob?

A function can be implemented in two ways in Lua. The most common method is to provide the keyword function then the function name:

function *funtionName* ()

   body or list of commands

end

Example

```
function showMessage()
  print("Hello, Lua!")
end
```

The second method is to assign the function to a variable:

functionName = **function()**

  body or list of commands

end

Example

```
showMessage = function ()
  print("Hello, Lua!")
end
```

Note that the function name, showMessage follows the same rules as creating a variable name:

> ➤ A variable can be any combination of letters, numbers, or underscores

- ➤ A variable must not begin with a number

- ➤ A variable cannot contain a space or any symbol except underscore

- ➤ Variables are case-sensitive. myVariable is not the same as MyVariable

It is good practice to indent all of the commands in the function to make the program more readable and show that the commands are a part of the function. Generally, one tab or five spaces are the standard for indentation.

Functions can return values to the calling command using the **return** command. Return values allow functions to provide results or computed values to the calling code.

Introduction to Arguments and Parameters

In Lua, we use parameters to define variables within a function's definition, and arguments refer to the actual data passed to those parameters from the calling routine or command. To clarify these terms, let's examine the following example:

```
-- Parameter: x   <- received by the function
-- Argument: 5    <- sent from program command

function multiplyByTwo(x)
    return x * 2
end

local result = multiplyByTwo(5) -- Passing the argument
```

```
5 to the parameter x
print(result)

Output
10
```

In this example, x is the parameter in our multiplyByTwo function, and 5 is the argument we pass to that parameter. The function then returns the value of x multiplied by 2, giving us a result of 10.

Passing Arguments and Receiving Parameters

Let's now explore various scenarios of passing arguments and receiving parameters in Lua functions. We'll expand upon the provided example and explain each case in more detail.

Basic Arguments and Parameters

```
function greet(name)
  print("Hello, " .. name .. "!")
end

greet("Alice")

Output
Hello, Alice!
```

In this basic example, we define a function called greet with a parameter name. When we call the function with the argument "Alice", it concatenates the argument with the greeting message and prints it to the console.

Storing Return Values

```
function calculateSum(a, b)
  return a + b
end

local result = calculateSum(3, 4)
print(result)
```

Output
7

Here, we have a function called calculateSum that takes two parameters, a and b. It adds the values of a and b together and returns the result. We store the return value in the variable result and print it to the console.

Declaring Default Values

Sometimes, we might want to provide default values for our parameters to handle cases when an argument is not provided.

```
function greet(name)
  if name == nil then
    name = "stranger"
  end
  print("Hello, " .. name .. "!")
end

greet()          -- Output: Hello, stranger!
greet("Bob")  -- Output: Hello, Bob!
```

In this modified greet function, if the name argument is not provided or is nil, we assign it the default value of "stranger".

Multiple Return Values

Lua functions can return multiple values. The returned values can be stored in multiple variables or used directly.

Example:

```
function rectangleProperties(width, height)
    local area = width * height
    local perimeter = 2 * (width + height)
    return area, perimeter
end

local area, perimeter = rectangleProperties(4, 6)
print(area, perimeter)
```

Output
24   20

In this example, we define a function called rectangleProperties that calculates the area and perimeter of a rectangle based on its width and height. The function returns both values as separate return values. We store these values in the variables area and perimeter respectively and print them to the console.

Return statements can exist anywhere within a function. Though, it only makes sense to provide a 'return' statement at the end of a code block, as any expressions that exist after a 'return' statement will not be evaluated. Lua even insists on this by raising an error if a 'return' statement is not found at the end of its parent code block.

Example:

```
function addNum( num1, num2 )
        result = num1 + num2
        return result
        print ('I will never be reached')
end

print ( addNum( 1, 2 ) )
```

Output
'end' expected (to close 'function' at line 1) near 'print'

A return command is only needed if you are returning a value to the calling statement.

Variable Scope

When you declare a variable inside of a function, the variable is only available inside that function. Think of it like light. Outside, we have sunlight, and it is everywhere. If I walk into a building, I still have sunlight through the windows. Sunlight is like a global variable; it is everywhere.

A local variable that is declared at the beginning of a file like main.lua is available anywhere in main.lua. It is local to main.lua. This is like turning on a light switch that turns on all the lights in a house. If I declare a local variable inside a function, it is only available inside that function. More like a table lamp; it is only usable on the table.

myGlobalVariable = "Lua is great"
is a global variable and could be used anywhere in our program (i.e., it is not declared using the keyword 'local').

local **myLocalVariable** = "I am a local variable"
is only used in the file (like main.lua) that it was created.

local function myFunction()
    local **anotherLocalVariable** = "I am in a function"
    end
is only usable inside the function. Once we are done with the function or if we call the variable **anotherLocalVariable** outside of the function, it will return a nil value, which could crash your program.

It is a best practice to always declare your variables at the beginning of the file or function if they will be used throughout the file. By declaring them at the beginning of the file, you will have the use of the variable everywhere in your file. If you need a temporary variable inside a function to do a calculation, that's fine, that's why we have them.

Best Practices:

> ➤ Always prefer using local variables over global variables whenever possible.

> ➤ Localizing variables and functions improves code readability, maintainability, and reduces the risk of conflicts.

> ➤ Avoid relying too heavily on global variables, as they can lead to unexpected behavior in complex programs.

Conclusion

Functions play a vital role in Lua programming by allowing us to organize and reuse code effectively. With the ability to accept parameters and return values, functions offer flexibility and enable powerful programming techniques. By understanding the concepts covered in this chapter, you are well-equipped to create functions, utilize parameters, and handle return values in Lua. Remember to adhere to best practices, such as localizing variables and minimizing the use of global variables, to improve code quality and maintainability.

Questions

1. What is a function in Lua?

2. How can functions help in organizing code?

3. What are the two ways to create a function in Lua?

4. How should you name your functions and why is it important to avoid naming conflicts?

5. How can indentation be used to enhance the readability of functions?

6. What are parameters in a function, and how are they declared?

7. How can a function return a value back to the calling code?

8. Can a function return multiple values in Lua? How are they handled?

9. Explain the concept of variable scope and the difference between local and global variables.

10. What risks or conflicts can arise from excessive use of global variables?

Exercises

1. Create a function named greetUser that takes a name parameter and prints a personalized greeting message.

2. Write a function called calculateArea that accepts the length and width of a rectangle as parameters and returns its area.

3. Create a function called convertToCelsius that converts a temperature from Fahrenheit to Celsius.

Chapter 6: Decisions in Lua

In this chapter, we will explore the powerful if-then command structure in Lua, which allows us to make decisions and execute specific code based on different conditions. The if-then structure in Lua is similar to what you'll find in other scripting and programming languages. It is used to handle various situations where you need the program to perform specific actions or execute particular code within your application.

Learning Objectives:

- ➤ Understand the basic structure of if-then statements in Lua

- ➤ Learn how to use comparison operators in if-then structures

- ➤ Explore the usage of logical operators (and, or, not) in if-then statements

- ➤ Apply nested if-then structures for complex decision-making

- ➤ Discover the purpose and applications of the select command in Lua

Simple If-Then Statements

The if-then structure consists of four main parts: the if command, the comparison to be evaluated, the keyword "then" followed by the code to be executed if the condition is true, and the keyword "end" to mark the end of the if-then structure.

if *Boolean expression* **then**
    one or more statements/commands
end

Lua provides several comparison operators such as equals (==), less than (<), greater than (>), not equals (~=), less than or equal to (<=), greater than or equal to (>=), and more.

Let's consider an example to understand the if-then structure better. Suppose we have a variable called "count" initialized as 0. We can use the if-then structure to perform different actions based on the value of "count."

Example:

```lua
local count = 0

if count == 1 then
   print("Count is equal to one.")
end

if count <= 1 then
   print("Count is less than or equal to one.")
end

if count >= 1 then
   print("Count is greater than or equal to one.")
end

if count ~= 1 then
```

```
    print("Count is not equal to one.")
end
```

In the above example, the code inside the first if statement will not be executed because the value of "count" is not equal to 1. However, the second if statement will print "Count is less than or equal to one" since count is indeed less than or equal to 1.

Learning Tip: *Remember that using a single equal sign (=) is used for assignment in Lua, while two equal signs (==) are used for equality comparison.*

Nested If-Then and Else Statements

In Lua, we can create nested if statements, where an if-then structure is nested within another if-then structure. This allows us to handle more complex decision-making scenarios. It is essential to use proper indentation and correctly balance the if and end statements to maintain code readability.

Consider the following example:

```
local count = 0
local answer = "yes"

if count == 0 then
   if answer == "yes" then
      print("Nested if: Count is zero and answer is
yes.")
   end
```

```
else
   print("Nested if: Count is not zero.")
end

Output
Nested if: Count is zero and answer is yes.
```

In the above example, the first if statement checks if count is equal to 0 (If-then commands have been bolded to the script easier to read).

If this condition is true, it goes inside the nested if statement to check if the answer is "yes." If both conditions are true, it executes the code inside the nested if statement and prints "Nested if: Count is zero and answer is yes."

If the first if statement's condition is false, it executes the code inside the else block, printing "Nested if: Count is not zero."

Nested if statements allow us to handle more complex situations and perform actions based on multiple conditions. However, be cautious not to create deeply nested structures, as they can quickly become difficult to read and understand. It's always a good practice to balance the **if** and **end** statements correctly to avoid syntax errors.

Logical Operators in If-Then Structures

In Lua, logical operators (and, or, not) allow us to combine conditions and create more complex if-then structures. These operators help us handle situations where multiple conditions need to be satisfied or where a condition needs to be negated.

The logical operator "and" returns true if both conditions on its left and right side are true. If either condition is false, it returns false. The logical operator "or" returns true if at least one of the conditions on its left or right side is true. It only returns false if both conditions are false. The logical operator "not" negates the result of a condition. If the condition is true, "not" returns false, and if the condition is false, "not" returns true.

Consider an example to see how logical operators work in if-then structures:

```
local score = 80
local grade = "A"

if score >= 90 and grade == "A" then
    print("Congratulations! You achieved an A grade
with a score above or equal to 90.")
end

if score >= 90 or grade == "A" then
    print("You either scored above or equal to 90 or
achieved an A grade.")
end

if not (score < 60) then
    print("You passed the exam!")
```

```

You either scored above or equal to 90 or achieved
an A grade.
You passed the exam!
```

In the above example, the first if statement checks if the score is greater than or equal to 90 **and** if the grade is "A." If both conditions are true, it executes the code inside the if statement.

The second if statement checks if the score is greater than **or** equal to 90 or if the grade is "A." If at least one of the conditions is true, it executes the code inside the if statement.

The third if statement uses the "**not**" operator to check if the score is not less than 60. If the condition is true (i.e., the score is greater than or equal to 60), it executes the code inside the if statement.

Learning Tip: Use parentheses to clarify the order of evaluation when combining logical operators in complex if-then structures.

Logical operators in Lua provide a way to combine conditions and create more sophisticated if-then structures. By using "and," "or," and "not," we can handle complex scenarios and make our code more versatile. Keep in mind the order of evaluation and use parentheses when needed. In the next section, we will explore the concept of else-if statements and how they expand our decision-making capabilities.

Else-If Statements

In Lua, else-if statements allow us to evaluate multiple conditions sequentially until a condition evaluates to true. This construct is useful when we have a series of conditions to check and want to perform specific actions based on the first condition that is true.

Here is the structure of an else-if statement in Lua:

```
if condition1 then
  -- code to execute if condition1 is true
elseif condition2 then
  -- code to execute if condition2 is true
elseif condition3 then
  -- code to execute if condition3 is true
else
  -- code to execute if none of the conditions are true
end
```

The conditions are evaluated sequentially, and the first condition that evaluates to true triggers the execution of the corresponding code block. If none of the conditions are true, the code inside the else block is executed.

Let's consider an example to understand else-if statements better:

```
local num = 5

if num < 0 then
    print("The number is negative.")
elseif num > 0 then
    print("The number is positive.")
else
    print("The number is zero.")
end
```

Output
The number is positive.

In the above example, if the number is less than 0, the code inside the first if block executes and prints "The number is negative." If the number is greater than 0, the code inside the elseif block executes and prints "The number is positive." If neither of these conditions is true, the code inside the else block executes and prints "The number is zero."

Else-if statements in Lua enable us to evaluate multiple conditions sequentially and perform specific actions based on the first condition that evaluates to true. They provide a more efficient way to handle complex decision-making scenarios. Make sure to order your conditions appropriately to ensure accurate evaluation.

Conclusion

In this chapter on Lua scripting, we explored the fundamentals of decision-making using if-then structures. We learned how to use if statements to execute code based on a condition's evaluation. We also discussed nested if statements, which allow us to handle more complex scenarios with multiple conditions. Next, we explored logical operators (and, or, not) that enhance decision-making by combining conditions. Lastly, we examined else-if statements, which provide a sequential evaluation of multiple conditions. By mastering these concepts, you can create versatile and efficient code to solve real-world problems.

Questions

1. What is the purpose of an if statement?

2. How do you define a nested if statement?

3. What is the difference between the logical operators "and" and "or"?

4. How does the logical operator "not" work?

5. What is the benefit of using else-if statements?

6. Can you have multiple else blocks in an if-then structure?

7. How are conditions evaluated in else-if statements?

8. How can you combine logical operators to create complex conditions?

9. Why is proper indentation important in nested if statements?

10. What is the role of parentheses in if-then structures?

Exercises

1. Write a Lua script that checks if a given number is even or odd and prints an appropriate message.

2. Write a Lua function that accepts three numbers as parameters and returns the largest of the three.

3. Implement a Lua script that calculates the grade for a given score according to the following rules: 90-100 is an A, 80-89 is a B, 70-79 is a C, 60-69 is a D, and below 60 is an F.

4. Develop a Lua program that takes a given age and prints different messages based on the following conditions: if age is less than 18, print "You are a minor." If age is between 18 and 65 (inclusive), print "You are an adult." If age is greater than 65, print "You are a senior citizen."

Chapter 7: Loops in Lua

In Lua, the for loop is a powerful tool for repeating a segment of code a specific number of times. It is especially useful when you know exactly how many iterations you need. Let's explore how the for loop works in Lua.

Learning Objectives

By the end of this chapter, you will be able to:

➢ Understand the concept and importance of loops in Lua scripting.

➢ Differentiate between the three main types of loops in Lua.

➢ Utilize for loops to repeat code a specific number of times, specifying the starting number, ending number, and step number.

➢ Choose the appropriate loop structure based on the requirements of your code.

➢ Use loops effectively to iterate over data structures, perform calculations, and control program flow.

Loops are also commonly used to control the flow of your program. Oftentimes we will have the need to do a set of commands multiple times or until some condition is met. Loops provide the means to accomplish these repetitive tasks. There are three ways to create a loop: while-do, repeat-until, and for-next. We will examine for-do loop first, as it is the simplest to understand.

for-do

The for-do loop (often referred to as the for-next loop) is used when we want to execute a block of code a known number of times.

for *name = start number, end number* [, step] **do**
    block
end

name - When starting a for-next loop, the first required item is a temporary variable *name* to store the number the loop is on. This can be any variable name, but should not be a variable that you are using elsewhere in your program.

Start number – any number or variable that holds a numeric value.

End number - any number or variable that holds a numeric value.

Step - (Optional) The increment for counting. Example: -1 to count down, 2 to count by evens or odds, 10 to count by 10, etc.

Examples:

```
for count1 = 1, 5 do  -- Count from 1 to 5 and print
the result
```

```
    print (count1)
end
```

Output
```
1
2
3
4
5
```

```
for count = 0, 10, 2 do  -- Count from 0 to 10 by 2's,
print the result
    print (count)
end
```

Output
```
0
2
4
6
8
10
```

```
for counter = 10, 1, -1 do  -- Count down from 10 to
1, print the result
    print (counter)
end
```

Output
```
10
```

```
9
8
7
6
5
4
3
2
1
```

while-do

The while-do loop repeats a block of code until a Boolean expression is no longer true. If the condition is false on the first loop of the while-do, then the block of code within the loop will never be run.

while *Boolean expression* **do**

   block

end

Example:

```
count = 0
while (count < 10 ) do
    print (count)
    count = count + 1
end

Output
0
```

```
1
2
3
4
5
6
7
8
9
```

Notice that the output only includes 0 to 9. When count is equal to 10, the condition is no longer true, so the loop stops running.

repeat-until

Similar to the while-do loop, repeat-until loop repeats a block of code until a condition becomes true. The repeat-until will always run the block of code at least once since the Boolean expression evaluation happens at the end of the loop.

repeat

   block

until Boolean *expression*

Example:

```
count = 0
repeat
    print (count)
```

```
      count = count + 1
until (count > 5)

Output
0
1
2
3
4
5
```

Learning Tip: *If you need to keep track of how many loops have happened in a while-do or repeat-until, you can add a variable to the block of code that adds 1 each time the block repeats: e.g. counter = counter + 1*

Nested Loops

When you place one type of loop inside another loop, it is called a nested loop. When a nested loop executes, every time the outside (or first) loop does one loop, the inside loop will loop until it completes its required loops.

You can mix loop types; a while loop can be placed in a for loop.

Example:

```
for outsideloop = 1, 3 do  -- outside loop
    print (outsideloop)
      for insideloop = 4, 1, -1 do   -- inside loop
```

```
        print (insideloop)
      end
end
```

Output
1 – outside loop
4 – inside loop
3 – inside loop
2 – inside loop
1 – inside loop
2 – outside loop
4 – inside loop
3 – inside loop
2 – inside loop
1 – inside loop
3 - outside loop
4 – inside loop
3 – inside loop
2 – inside loop
1 – inside loop

Infinite Loops

An infinite loop is usually created by accident. It is the situation when the condition that will stop or complete the loop are never met:

```
count  = 0
while (count < 10) do
   counter = counter + 1
end
```

As you can see with the example above, **count** will never increase in value, as the variable being changed is **counter**. Situations like this will cause your app to lock-up and potentially crash.

To avoid infinite loops, always double check that, at some point, the condition that will end the loop will occur.

Conclusion

In Lua, loops are essential for executing code repeatedly and controlling the flow of your program. By understanding the concept and importance of loops, differentiating between the three main types of loops (for, while, and repeat), and utilizing them effectively, you can enhance your Lua scripting skills.

The for loop is particularly useful when you know the exact number of iterations required. It allows you to repeat a segment of code a specific number of times by specifying the starting number, ending number, and step number.

The while-do loop repeats a block of code until a condition becomes false. We learned that the loop will only execute if the initial condition is true, and we should ensure that the condition is eventually resolved to avoid infinite loops.

The repeat-until loop is similar to the while-do loop but guarantees that the block of code will run at least once. The loop continues until a condition becomes true.

We also discussed nested loops, which occur when one loop is placed inside another loop. Nested loops allow you to perform more complex iterations, with the inner loop executing for each iteration of the outer loop.

By mastering loops in Lua, you can simplify repetitive tasks, iterate over data structures, perform calculations, and control program flow efficiently. Remember to choose the appropriate loop structure based on your code's requirements and always consider the conditions that will end the loop.

Questions

1. What is the purpose of using loops in Lua scripting?

2. What are the three main types of loops in Lua?

3. Can the step value in a for loop be negative? Give an example.

4. How can you count from 1 to 10 using a for loop in Lua?

5. Explain the output of the code snippet: "for count = 0, 10, 2 do print(count) end".

6. How does a while-do loop differ from a for loop in Lua?

7. What is the purpose of the Boolean expression in a while-do loop?

8. Describe the structure of a repeat-until loop in Lua.

9. How does a repeat-until loop differ from a while-do loop?

10. Give an example of a situation where you would use a repeat-until loop.

Exercises

1. Write a Lua for loop that counts from 1 to 20, printing each number in the process.

2. Create a Lua repeat-until loop that prints the squares of the numbers from 1 to 10.

3. Write a Lua nested loop that prints the multiplication table for numbers from 1 to 5. For example, the output should be:
   1 2 3 4 5
   2 4 6 8 10
   3 6 9 12 15
   4 8 12 16 20
   5 10 15 20 25

4. Using a for loop, calculate and print the sum of the numbers from 1 to 100.

Part II:
Intermediate Concepts of Lua

Chapter 8: Input & Output

In this chapter, we will explore file input and output (I/O) as well as standard I/O using the Lua scripting language. The I/O library in Lua provides six essential tools that allow us to interact with files and perform input/output operations. These tools include read and write operations, which enable us to receive information from the keyboard and output it to the display. Additionally, we will learn about file manipulation and how to work with different file modes.

Learning Objectives

- Understand standard input and output mechanisms in Lua, including interaction with the keyboard and display/terminal window.

- Differentiate between implicit and explicit file input and output operations in Lua.

- Explore file manipulation and the use of different file modes for reading and writing files.

- Learn how to use the I/O library for implicit file operations and the file library for explicit file operations.

- Gain proficiency in reading and writing data to text files and binary files in Lua.

Standard Input and Output

The I/O library provides standard input and output mechanisms for interacting with the keyboard, display, and files. The standard in (stdin) receives information from the keyboard, while the standard out (stdout) outputs information to the display/terminal window.

Example:

```
io.write("How old are you? ")
local answer = io.read()
print("You entered: " .. answer)
```

Output
How old are you? [user input]
You entered: [user input]

In this example, we use **io.write** to ask a question and **io.read** to store the user's response in the variable answer. The print function is used to display the user's input.

Output with Print

Instead of using io.write for outputting to the display, we generally use the print function. Print automatically converts values to strings and provides convenient formatting options, such as using commas for tabs and other formatting techniques. It simplifies the process of debugging and displaying information.

Let's compare io.write and print:

```
io.write("Hello, ")
io.write("Lua!\n")  -- \n for a new line

print("Hello,", "Lua!")

Output
Hello, Lua!
Hello, Lua!
```

As you can see, print automatically concatenates the arguments and adds a new line at the end; much easier than using **io.write** to output information to the terminal window!

File Input and Output

I am sure that you have noticed that many apps and games take a few seconds (or even minutes) to load. This is primarily due to needing to load a large quantity of data or graphics into memory. By storing data in external files, we are able to accomplish several important features.

If security is a concern, either because we are using personal data from those who use our app or the need to safeguard proprietary information, we can encrypt data files making it much more difficult to hack or steal the information. If the data is kept unencrypted, it can be accessed by others.

If I have created a complex game or application, I will usually need to load a lot of information. While I can program all of the level information into the game, using that approach makes it much more difficult to provide updates, bug fixes, or new levels to the game without resubmitting the app for app store approval. By storing as much information as possible in external files, I can download updates to my users without needing to go through the approval process again.

Implicit vs. Explicit Files

Lua has two different types of file input and output: implicit and explicit.

Implicit file operations use standard, predefined files for file input and output. By default this is stdin (standard in), stdout (standard out), and stderr (error reporting). While at first consideration it might seem strange to think of the terminal output as a 'file,' it is by traditional Computer Science considerations. In the 'old' days of computer usage (i.e. pre-1980s), any operation that wrote or read information to or from a location was file input or output (file I/O). In the early days of mainframe computer systems, to be able to output information to a terminal was very similar to writing data to a file or sending the information to a printer. Thus, as programming languages have developed, reading or writing to the terminal window is still considered a file I/O operation. Consider it a long winded way of doing a print command.

Explicit file operations allow the reading and writing of typical (i.e. not terminal) files including text files and binary files. For the majority of your file operations you will be using the explicit file tools. The file libraries are differentiated for the two types of file manipulation. The IO library is for implicit, and the file library is for explicit.

Implicit Read

io.type(*filehandle*) – checks whether the file handle is valid. Returns the string "file" if the file is open, "closed file" if the file is closed (not in use), and nil if the object is not a file handle.

io.open(*filename_path [, mode]*) – opens a file for reading or writing in string (default) or binary mode. Will create the file if it doesn't already exist. Modes: "r" – read; "w" – write; "a" – append; "r+" – update, all previous data preserved; "w+" – update, all previous data erased; "a+" – append update, all previous data preserved, writing allowed at the end of file. Mode string can include "b" for binary mode.

io.input(*[file]*) – sets the standard input file (default is Corona Terminal)

io.lines(*filename*) – opens the given file in read mode. Returns an iterator (counter) that each time it is called, returns a new line from the file.

io.read(*[fmt]*) – reads the file set by io.input based upon the read format. Generally used with Corona Terminal. Use file:read to for files.

io.close() – closes the open file.

io.tmpfile() – creates an empty, temporary file for reading and writing.

Explicit Read

file:read(*[fmt1] [,fmt2] [, ...]*) – reads a file according to the given format. Available formats include: "*n" – reads a number; "*a" – reads the whole file starting at the current position; "*l" – reads the next line (default); number – reads a string with up to the number of characters.

file:lines() – iterates through the file, returning a new line each time it is called.

file:seek(*[mode] [, offset]*) – sets and gets the file position, measured from the beginning of the file. Can be used to get the current file position or set the file position.

file:close() – Close the open file.

Implicit Write

io.output(*[file]*) – sets the standard output file (default is Corona Terminal).

io.write(*arg1 [, arg2] [, ...]*) – writes the argument to the file. The arguments must be a string or number.

io.flush() – forces the write of any pending io.write commands to the io.output file.

Explicit Write

file:setvbuf(*mode [, size]*) – sets the buffering mode for file writes. Available modes include: "no" – no buffering (can affect app performance); "full" – output only performed when buffer is full or flush; "line" – buffering occurs until a newline is output. Size argument is in bytes.

file:write(*arg1 [, arg2] [, ...]*) – writes the value of each argument to the file. Arguments must be strings or numbers.

file:flush() – forces the write of any pending file:write commands to the file.

Example: Reading & Writing to a File

In the following examples, we will create simple apps to write and read data to a text file that will be stored in the project folder of the app. We will use both implicit and explicit API calls to accomplish our write and read.

One of the first decisions you must make when preparing to write a file is if you need to preserve information that was previously written to the file. When opening the file to write, you must decide if you are overwriting/erasing all previous information ("w"), or appending to previously written data ("a"). When opening a file for writing or appending, if the file does not exist, it will be created.

To keep things simple, I am going to assume that I am not concerned about previously saved files. So, I will use the "w" mode to create or overwrite any previous file.

```
-- Set the file name to write
myExampleFile = "ch8Write"

-- open/create the file
local myFile = io.open( myExampleFile, "w" )

myFile:write("Hi Mom! I made a file\n")
myFile:flush()
io.close(myFile)
```

When you are finished writing information to the file, you should always flush the data. This will ensure that everything has been written to the file before it is closed.

Now we will add the code to read the data from the file and display it to the screen. After verifying that the file exists, we can load all the file's contents by using the "*a" parameter.

```
-- check that the file was created
myFile = io.open( myExampleFile, "r" )
if myFile then
   -- the file exists, read the data
   local contents = myFile:read( "*a" )
   local myOutput ="Contents of \n" .. myExampleFile
.. "\n" .. contents
   io.close(myFile)
   print(myOutput)
end

Output
Contents of
ch8Write
Hi Mom! I made a file
```

Now that we have successfully created a file, let's look at an example of a file that can be appended.

Example: Appending & Reading from a File
Building on project 8.0, we will now use the append command. The advantage of this command is data will be added each time we run the program. Thus, if we run the app multiple times, it will continue to add new lines of data. To start using append, we only need to replace the "w" with "a" in the initial open command:

```
-- Set the file name to write
myExampleFile = "ch8Write"

-- open/create the file
local myFile = io.open( myExampleFile, "a" )

myFile:write("Hi Dad! I made a file \n")
myFile:flush()
io.close(myFile)

-- check that the file was created
myFile = io.open( myExampleFile, "r" )
if myFile then
   -- the file exists, read the data
   local contents = myFile:read( "*a" )
   local myOutput ="Contents of \n" .. myExampleFile
.. "\n" .. contents
   io.close(myFile)
   print(myOutput)
end
```

Output
Contents of
ch8Write
Hi Mom! I made a file
Hi Dad! I made a file

By adding the "\n" to the end of our write command, we can easily see the additional lines of text since \n forces a new line to the display.

Run this app a few times to see the impact of append.

File Modes

When working with files, we have different modes available to us: read, write, binary read, and binary write. The read and write modes create text files, which store basic ASCII text. On the other hand, binary read and write modes are used when dealing with files containing binary information.

Let's see how this works with an example:

```lua
local file = io.open("data.bin", "wb")
file:write("Hello, Lua!")
file:close()

local readFile = io.open("data.bin", "rb")
local content = readFile:read("*all")
print("File content:", content)
readFile:close()
```

Output
File content: Hello, Lua!

In this example, we create a file named "data.bin" using io.open with the "wb" mode, which stands for write binary. We write the text "Hello, Lua!" to the file and then close it. Next, we open the same file in binary read mode ("rb"), read the entire content using readFile:read("*all"), and print it.

The binary read and write mode is very important should you need to work with binary data such as a database or other binary file formats.

Conclusion

In this chapter, we delved into file input and output (I/O) as well as standard I/O using Lua. We explored the essential tools provided by the I/O library in Lua that enable us to interact with files and perform input/output operations. We learned about standard input and output mechanisms, the use of print for outputting to the display, and the advantages it offers over io.write. Additionally, we discussed file manipulation, differentiating between implicit and explicit file operations, and how to work with file modes. By understanding these concepts, we can effectively read and write data from and to files in Lua, opening up possibilities for data storage, security, and application updates.

Questions

1. What are the standard input and output mechanisms in Lua?

2. How does the print function differ from io.write when outputting to the display?

3. What are the advantages of storing data in external files?

4. Why is storing information in external files beneficial for providing updates to an application or game?

5. What are the differences between implicit and explicit file operations in Lua?

6. What are the different file modes available for opening a file in Lua?

7. How can you read an entire file in Lua using the io library?

8. How can you iterate through a file and read it line by line in Lua using the file library?

9. How can you write data to a file in Lua using the io library?

10. How can you set the buffering mode for file writes in Lua using the file library?

Exercises

1. Write a Lua program that asks the user to enter their name and saves it to a file named "names.txt".

2. Modify the previous program to read the contents of the "names.txt" file and display them on the screen.

3. Create a Lua function that takes a filename as input and counts the number of lines in that file.

4. Write a Lua program that appends the current date and time to a file named "log.txt" every time it is executed.

5. Create a Lua function that takes a filename as input and checks if the file exists.

6. Create a Lua function that takes a filename and a string as input and appends the string to the end of the file.

Chapter 9: Data Structures: Tables and the Table Library

In this chapter we are going to begin working with Tables. Tables have become a critical part of application development. Tables are one of the simplest ways to store large quantities of data.

Learning Objectives
In our examination of tables we will:
- Clarify the terms table and array
- Examine the tools available for tables
- Create one and two dimensional tables

Tables vs. Arrays
The term table has many different meanings in programming. It can be used to refer to an array (which is the common usage in Lua), a grid layout (like a spreadsheet), or a table view (popularized by Apple for developing data-intensive applications) - sometimes also referred to as a list view.

Introducing Tables
When teaching programming, one of the dividing lines between the novice programmer and the intermediate programmer is the understanding of the concept of

arrays. If you can understand this concept, you will be set for a whole new world of programming concepts and items that you can create.

I have always found it easiest to conceptualize an array by picturing a single column in a spreadsheet. If I wanted to create an array of the first names of students in my class, it might look like:

myStudents =

| Joe |
| Jean |
| Fred |
| Cindy |
| Mary |

In this example, I have 5 students. All of the students are stored in one variable: myStudents. Because they are all stored as one variable, I am able to work with them as a group of records.

Each part or row of the array is referred to as an element. Thus "Joe" is the value of the first element of the array.

To create an array in Lua, you use curly brackets in the variable declaration:

local myStudents = {}

You can also declare the contents of the array:

```
local myStudents = {"Joe", "Jean", "Fred", "Cindy",
"Mary"}
```

Note: If you want Lua to treat the names as strings, they have to be in quotations; else they will be treated like variables.

Now we can easily access each of the students using a for...do loop:

```
local myStudents = {"Joe", "Jean", "Fred", "Cindy",
"Mary"}
for count1 = 1, 5 do
        print (myStudents[count1])
end
```

Output
Joe
Jean
Fred
Cindy
Mary

Table API

We have several useful commands that can be used through the table API:

- ➤ table.concat(*array [, string, number1, number2]*) – concatenates the elements of an array to form a string. Optionally, you can pass a string to be inserted between the values (such as ", "). Number1 and number2 refer to the index of the elements to be concatenated. Number1 must be less than number2. If omitted, number1 will be the first element in the table and number2 will be the last element.
- ➤ table.insert(*array, [position,] value*) - inserts the provided value into a table. If a position is supplied, the value is inserted before the element currently in that position.
- ➤ table.remove(*array [, position]*) – removes the table element in the supplied position. If a position is not provided, then the last element in the array is removed.
- ➤ table.sort(*array [, comparison]*) – sorts the table element into a given order, updating the table to the new sorted order. By default, < (less than or alphabetical order) is used. If a comparison is supplied, it must be a function that receives two table elements.

Let's examine the usage of each of these API commands:

Concatenation

When concatenating an array, you are creating a string using the elements within the array:

```
local myStudents = {"Joe", "Jean", "Fred", "Cindy",
```

```
"Mary"}
print (table.concat(myStudents, ","))
```

Output
Joe, Jean, Fred, Cindy, Mary

Insert

Inserts a new element into an array. If a position is not provided as an argument, the new element will be added as the last element of the array. If a position is provided, the new element will be inserted before the element previously at that index (i.e., what was the second element becomes the third element).

```
local myStudents = {"Joe", "Jean", "Fred", "Cindy",
"Mary"}
table.insert(myStudents, 2, "Jeff")
print(table.concat(myStudents, ", ")
```

Output
Joe, Jeff, Jean, Fred, Cindy, Mary

Remove

The remove API deletes from the array the element at the provided index position. If no index position is provided, the last element will be deleted from the array.

```
local myStudents = {"Joe", "Jeff", "Jean", "Fred",
"Cindy", "Mary"}
table.remove(myStudents, 2)
print(table.concat(myStudents, ", ")


-- Output:
Joe, Jean, Fred, Cindy, Mary
```

Sort

The sort API command sorts the table into alphabetical or numerical order if an operand is not provided. If a different sort order is needed, you will need to supply a function that will return true or false if the sort condition is not met.

For example, if you wanted to sort an array in reverse-alphabetical order (i.e., >), then you would need a program such as:

```
local myStudents = {"Joe", "Jean", "Fred", "Cindy",
"Mary"}

local function compare(a, b)
    return a > b
end

table.sort(myStudents, compare)

print(table.concat(myStudents, ", ")
```

Output
Mary, Joe, Jean, Fred, Cindy

Sort will pass the elements two at a time for our compare function to determine if the first element is greater than the second element. Thus, in the first instance, Joe and Jean will be passed. Since "Joe" is greater than "Jean" (at least alphabetically), the compare function will return the value TRUE, which tells the sort API it doesn't need to do anything. In the case of Joe and Mary, it will return FALSE, causing the sort API to place "Mary" before "Joe".

Flexibility of Lua Tables

Lua tables are very flexible in the content that they can contain. They are commonly used to handle events and a return from a function. In most programming languages, arrays must be of a specific data type such as integer, string, floating decimal, Boolean, etc. In Lua, we have more flexibility. Lua array tables can be heterogeneous, i.e., they can be of any data type. They can contain any type of data except nil.

Once you have declared a Lua array table, you can also use it to represent records or objects with field names. Once you have created your Lua table, you can create your own field names as needed by placing a period after the variable name, just like you would access a property for the variable such as the x or y location:

```
local myArray = {}
myArray.id = 1
myArray.myName = "Array 1"
myArray.x = 10
myArray.y = 50
```

You can also use a Lua array table to describe an object. For instance, if I was creating an RPG (Role Playing Game), I might create a player object such as:

```
local player1 = {}
player1.location = level
player1.class = "fighter"
player1.name = "Conan"
player1.weapon = "sword"
player1.health = 10
player1.image = display.newImage("player1.png")
```

Obviously, Lua tables are very flexible and can help organize your app data in many useful ways. All of this information is now associated with the variable player1 and can be accessed through its properties. Note that you can associate images, sounds, or even functions to an element of an array table.

Multi-dimensional Arrays

That takes care of a single or one-dimensional array/table, but what about multi-dimensional arrays? Yes, it is possible (and often necessary) to create arrays that are 2, 3, 4, or more dimensions! To keep it simple, we are just going to look at 2-dimensional arrays. The same concepts apply if you find yourself needing to build more complex arrays.

To create multi-dimensional array tables, you can assign an array table within an array table. To simplify working with multi-dimensional tables, I recommend that you always use a numeric index:

Project 10.1 Multi-dimensional Array

```
local myArray ={}
 myArray[1]={"Joe", "Jean", "Fred", "Cindy"}  -- first
name
 myArray[2] = {"Smith", "Smith", "Smith", "Smith"} –
last name
 myArray[3]={"142 Main", "163 South St."} -- address
 myArray[4]={} -- city
 myArray[5] = {} -- state
 myArray[6] = {} – zip code

for i = 1, 6 do
        for j = 1,4 do
                print (myArray[i][j])
        end
end
```

This creates a 2-dimensional array:

myArray =

Joe	Smith	142 Main			
Jean	Smith	163 South St.			
Fred	Smith				
Cindy	Smith				

Note: *How you choose to conceptualize the array is a matter of personal preference. In the first visual, I used a column to represent a 1-dimensional array. In this visual, I have instead used the first dimension to represent a row, with the second dimension representing the columns.*

Just like before, we have flexibility in what we can store within the Lua table. One warning: be very careful when storing certain information in any type of variable. Numbers such as telephone numbers, social security, driver's license, etc. should be treated as strings and not as numbers. In other words, storing 321-555-4651 is very different than "321-555-4651". The first number will be treated as a number and calculated resulting in -4,885. The second, since it is enclosed in quotes will be treated as a string and retain its original meaning.

To cycle through a more complex array such as what we have in our example, you need to use a nested loop:

```
for i = 1, 6 do
      for j = 1,4 do
            print (myArray[i][j])
      end
end
```

To access each dimension of an array, use a bracket for the index number. For example: If I have the command print(myArray[1][2]) the result will be Jean; the 1st column, 2nd row. As you can see, I did not fully populate the array. When the app runs, the empty elements will be returned as nil.

Summary

You now have a taste of working with arrays. Congratulations! This concept is what is generally considered to separate the beginner from the intermediate programmer! It will take some time to become comfortable working with arrays and tables, but you are now well on your way.

Questions

1. What are the different meanings of the term "table" in programming?

2. How would you create an array of the first names of students in Lua?

3. How can you access each element of an array using a loop in Lua?

4. What is the purpose of the table.concat function in Lua?

5. How would you insert a new element into an array at a specific position using the table.insert function?

6. What does the table.remove function do in Lua?

7. How can you sort the elements of an array in Lua using the table.sort function?

8. What is the default sort order used by the table.sort function?

9. How can you concatenate the elements of an array into a string using table.concat?

10. What are multi-dimensional arrays, and how are they created in Lua?

Exercises

1. Create a simple array showing exam scores for a class of 6 students: 85, 67, 92, 42, 99, 77. Using table.insert, add an additional score of 96.

2. Building on assignment 1, sort the array in ascending order.

3. Building on assignment 1, remove the 3rd element.

4. Create a lamp object that has the following properties:

    Color: blue   status: off   bulb: 60W   power: battery

Then write a function to change the lamp status to on if it is off, or off if it is on.

5. Create a two-dimensional array that shows 5 student's names in the first column and their current class grade (in percent) in the second column.

Chapter 10: Pairs and Ipairs

In Lua, the pairs and ipairs commands are essential tools known as generic for loops. These commands are frequently used in conjunction with tables to iterate over and process every item stored within the table. The ipairs command is used with ordered tables, while the pairs command is used for unordered tables. In this chapter, we will explore these commands in detail, along with relevant programming examples.

Learning Objectives

➤ Understand the purpose and functionality of the pairs and ipairs commands in Lua.

➤ Explain the difference between ordered and unordered tables.

➤ Explore the application of pairs and ipairs in multi-dimensional tables.

➤ Recognize the advantages of using pairs and ipairs for table manipulation.

➤ Appreciate the benefits of comprehensive table traversal.

➤ Understand how pairs and ipairs aid in troubleshooting and debugging by providing more informative output.

Understanding Keys and Values in Tables

Before we dive into the pairs and ipairs commands, let's examine the concept of keys and values in Lua tables. In Lua, a table is a collection of key-value pairs, where each value is associated with a unique key. The key represents the index or position of the value within the table. Unlike arrays, Lua tables are not restricted to a specific variable type, allowing you to store different types of information within the same table.

For example, consider the following table:

```
local myTable = {"hi", "hello", "world", 42,
"inconceivable"}
```

In this table, we have stored different elements (values) such as strings ("hi", "hello", "world"), a number (42), and another string ("inconceivable").

For this table, we are using a key that is based on the index. The first element (value), "hi" will have an index of 1, so the myTable[1] key has a value of "hi". In Lua, we are not restricted to only using the index, we can also create different types of keys for values.

Ordered Tables vs Unordered Table

In Lua, the terms "ordered table" and "unordered table" refer to different characteristics of tables based on how their elements are organized and accessed.

Ordered Table
> An ordered table is a table where the elements are indexed sequentially, starting from 1 and continuing in ascending order.
> The order of elements in an ordered table is determined by their index values, which correspond to their position within the table.
> Iterating over an ordered table guarantees that the elements will be processed in the same order as their indices.
> The ipairs command is typically used to iterate over and access elements in an ordered table.

Ordered Table Example:

```
local fruits = {"apple", "banana", "orange", "grape"}
```

In this example, we have an ordered table named fruits. The elements of the table are stored in a sequential manner with index values starting from 1 and increasing in ascending order.

You can access the elements of this ordered table using their indices. Here's an example of how you can retrieve and print the elements:

```
for i = 1, #fruits do
    print("Index:", i, "Fruit:", fruits[i])
end
```

Output

```
Index: 1       Fruit: apple
Index: 2       Fruit: banana
Index: 3       Fruit: orange
Index: 4       Fruit: grape
```

In the above code, we use a **for** loop to iterate over the indices of the fruits table. The loop starts from index 1 and goes up to the length of the table (#fruits), which gives us the total number of elements in the table. Within the loop, we access each element by its index (fruits[i]) and print it along with the corresponding index.

The order in which the elements are defined in the table determines the sequence in which they are accessed. In an ordered table, you can rely on the indices to retrieve the elements in a specific order.

Unordered Table:
- ➢ An unordered table, also known as a hash table or dictionary, does not have a specific order for its elements.
- ➢ The elements in an unordered table are stored based on their keys, which can be of any type (e.g., strings, numbers, etc.).
- ➢ The order in which elements are stored in an unordered table does not necessarily reflect the order in which they were added.
- ➢ Iterating over an unordered table does not guarantee a specific order for processing its elements.

➢ The pairs command is typically used to iterate over and access elements in an unordered table.

Unordered Table Example:

```lua
local student = {
  name = "John Doe",
  age = 20,
  grade = "A",
  major = "Computer Science"
}
```

In this example, we have an unordered table named student. The table contains key-value pairs where the keys represent attributes of a student (e.g., name, age, grade, major), and the corresponding values represent the specific information associated with each attribute.

```lua
print("Name:", student.name)
print("Age:", student.age)
print("Grade:", student.grade)
print("Major:", student.major)
```

Output
Name: John Doe
Age: 20
Grade: A
Major: Computer Science

In the above code, we use the keys (name, age, grade, major) to access the corresponding values stored in the student table.

Note that the order in which the key-value pairs are defined in the table does not affect how they are accessed. The pairs command can be used to iterate over the elements of an unordered table and perform operations on each key-value pair.

In summary, an ordered table maintains a specific sequence for its elements based on their index values, while an unordered table does not follow any particular sequence and stores elements based on their associated keys. Understanding the distinction between these two types of tables is important when choosing the appropriate iteration method and working with table data in Lua.

Using ipairs for Ordered Tables

The ipairs command is specifically designed to iterate over ordered tables. An ordered table is a table where the elements are indexed sequentially starting from 1.

Let's explore an example to understand how ipairs works with ordered tables:

```
local myTable = {"hi", "hello", "world", 42,
"inconceivable"}

for index, value in ipairs(myTable) do
    print("Index:", index, "Value:", value)
```

```

Index: 1        Value: hi
Index: 2        Value: hello
Index: 3        Value: world
Index: 4        Value: 42
Index: 5        Value: inconceivable
```

In this example, we use the ipairs command to iterate over the elements of the myTable table. The generic for loop assigns each index to the index variable and the corresponding value to the value variable. As the loop progresses, it prints the index and value for each element.

Exploring pairs for Unordered Tables

While **ipairs** works with **ordered** tables, the **pairs** command is used to iterate over **unordered** tables. Unordered tables do not guarantee a specific order for their elements. Let's consider an example to illustrate the usage of pairs with an unordered table:

```
local myTable = {
  name = "Joe",
  age = 12,
  seat = "B12",
  grade = 7,
  date = "May 12"
}
```

```
for key, value in pairs(myTable) do
    print("Key:", key, "Value:", value)
end
```

Output
Key: name	Value: Joe
Key: age	Value: 12
Key: seat	Value: B12
Key: grade	Value: 7
Key: date	Value: May 12

In this example, we have a table *myTable* with key-value pairs representing different attributes. The pairs command allows us to iterate over the table and access both the key and its corresponding value. As the loop progresses, it prints the key and value for each element.

Working with Multi-dimensional Tables

Lua supports multi-dimensional tables, which consist of nested tables or arrays. When dealing with multi-dimensional tables, the pairs and ipairs commands remain crucial for effective table traversal. The length operator (#) is often inadequate for determining the size of multi-dimensional tables, as it only provides the count of the first dimension.

Consider the following example of a multi-dimensional table:

```
local multiTable = {
```

```
    {1, 2, 3},
    {4, 5, 6},
    {7, 8, 9}
}

for index, subTable in ipairs(multiTable) do
    for subIndex, value in ipairs(subTable) do
        print("Index:", index, "Sub-index:", subIndex,
"Value:", value)
    end
end
```

Output
```
Index: 1        Sub-index: 1  Value: 1
Index: 1        Sub-index: 2  Value: 2
Index: 1        Sub-index: 3  Value: 3
Index: 2        Sub-index: 1  Value: 4
Index: 2        Sub-index: 2  Value: 5
Index: 2        Sub-index: 3  Value: 6
Index: 3        Sub-index: 1  Value: 7
Index: 3        Sub-index: 2  Value: 8
Index: 3        Sub-index: 3  Value: 9
```

In this example, we have a multi-dimensional table *multiTable* consisting of three sub-tables. By using nested loops with ipairs, we can traverse each sub-table and access its elements. The outer loop iterates over the primary table, while the inner loop iterates over each sub-table, printing the index, sub-index, and value for each element.

Benefits of Using pairs and ipairs

Pairs and ipairs are powerful tools for working with Lua tables. Here are a few reasons why they are invaluable for table manipulation:

> ➢ Comprehensive Table Traversal: Pairs and ipairs allow you to effortlessly iterate over every key-value pair within a table, regardless of its structure. This feature is particularly helpful when dealing with complex, multi-dimensional tables.
> ➢ Flexibility in Ordered and Unordered Tables: The use of ipairs and pairs enables you to handle both ordered and unordered tables effectively.
> ➢ Enhanced Troubleshooting: When examining the contents of a table during debugging or troubleshooting, pairs and ipairs provide a more informative and readable output compared to simple print statements. They allow you to easily comprehend the data stored within the table and identify any inconsistencies.

Conclusion

In this chapter, we explored the pairs and ipairs commands, which are crucial for working with Lua tables. The ipairs command is suitable for ordered tables, while the pairs command is used for unordered tables. We examined examples illustrating their usage and the benefits they offer when working with both simple and multi-dimensional tables. By leveraging these commands, you can efficiently traverse and process table data, making Lua a powerful scripting language for various applications.

Questions

1. What are the pairs and ipairs commands used for in Lua?

2. How does the ipairs command differ from the pairs command?

3. What is the difference between an ordered table and an unordered table?

4. How are elements stored in an ordered table?

5. How are elements stored in an unordered table?

6. What is the advantage of using pairs and ipairs for table manipulation?

7. What does it mean for a table to be multi-dimensional?

8. How can pairs and ipairs be used with multi-dimensional tables?

9. How can pairs and ipairs aid in troubleshooting and debugging?

10. How does the length operator (#) work with multi-dimensional tables?

Exercises

1. Create an ordered table named "colors" with elements representing 6 different colors. Print each color using ipairs.

2. Create an unordered table named "person" with key-value pairs representing personal information such as name, age, and address. Print each key-value pair using pairs.

3. Create a multi-dimensional table named "matrix" that represents a 3x3 matrix. Iterate over the matrix using nested ipairs loops and print each element.

4. Write a function that takes an ordered table as input and returns the sum of all its elements.

5. Write a program that creates an unordered table of student names and their corresponding grades. Calculate the average grade using pairs.

Chapter 11: Closure

In the previous chapters, we learned about functions in Lua scripting and how they help us manipulate data and perform specific tasks. Now, we're going to dive deeper into the concept of closures, a powerful feature of the Lua language. Closures allow us to create anonymous functions that can remember and access variables from their *enclosing* environment.

Learning Objectives

By the end of this chapter, you will be able to:

> Define the concept of closures in Lua scripting.

> Understand the benefits of using closures in programming.

> Create closures that encapsulate variables from their enclosing environment.

> Explain how closures reduce the number of parameters needed in function signatures.

> Apply closures to solve practical programming problems, such as delaying function execution.

> Recognize the flexibility provided by closures in adapting the behavior of functions based on variable conditions.

What are Closures?

Closures, in simple terms, are local functions that have the ability to access variables from the surrounding variable scope. While regular functions are standalone and operate independently, closures are dynamic and can "bake in" variables from their environment. This makes closures highly flexible and useful in many programming scenarios. Closures are anonymous functions. That means that the function is being stored as a variable and does not have a function name.

Let's look at an example:

```
function buildClosure(num)
   local closureValue = function()
      print(num)
   end
   return closureValue
end

test1 = buildClosure(22)
test2 = buildClosure(100)

print(test1())   -- outputs 22
print(test2())   -- outputs 100
```

In this example, the buildClosure function creates a closure (i.e. an anonymous function) and stores it in the variable closureValue. The closure is defined as an anonymous function that prints the value of the num variable. When we call buildClosure and assign its result to test1 and test2, we effectively create two closures that have different values for num. When we invoke these closures, they remember the value of num and print it.

Benefits of Using Closures

Closures provide several benefits when working with Lua scripting:

Encapsulation

Closures allow us to encapsulate related functionality within a single function. By bundling variables and code together, we can create self-contained units or objects of behavior that are easier to manage and reuse. This enhances the structure and modularity of our programs.

Reduced Parameter Count

Closures enable us to reduce the number of parameters needed in their signature. Instead of passing multiple arguments to a function, we can rely on variables in the enclosing environment. This simplifies the interface of the closure and makes it more intuitive to use.

Flexibility

With closures, we can adapt the behavior of a function based on conditions present during its creation. The closure's purpose can be defined by the variables it captures, allowing us to create highly customizable and flexible code. The calling code doesn't need to know the intricacies of these conditions, making the closure easier to work with.

Closure Examples

Now that we understand the benefits of closures, let's explore a practical example where closures can be applied effectively.

Imagine you're developing a tower defense game in Lua using Solar2D. You need a function to launch waves of enemies that attack the towers. However, you encounter a problem with the timer delay. The built-in timer.performWithDelay api in Solar2D immediately executes a secondary function instead of delaying it when additional information is passed alongside. To overcome this, closures can be employed.

Here's an example of how closures can help solve this problem:

```lua
function startWave(delay)
    local numWaves = 0

    local launchWave = function()
        numWaves = numWaves + 1
        print("Launching Wave " .. numWaves)
        -- Code to spawn enemies and attack towers
goes here
    end

    local timerClosure = function()
```

```
        launchWave()
        timer.performWithDelay(delay, timerClosure)
    end

    timer.performWithDelay(delay, timerClosure)
end

startWave(2000) -- Launches a new wave every 2
seconds
```

In this example, the startWave function creates two closures: launchWave and timerClosure. The launchWave closure increments the numWaves variable and prints a message when invoked. The timerClosure closure calls launchWave and sets up a timer to call itself with a delay. By utilizing closures, we ensure that the necessary delay is maintained when launching new waves, solving the problem we encountered.

Conclusion

Closures are a powerful feature of the Lua scripting language that allow us to create dynamic and flexible functions. By encapsulating variables and code within a closure, we can achieve greater modularity and reduce the complexity of our programs.
Understanding closures opens up new possibilities for creating efficient and adaptable code in Lua scripting.

Questions

1. What is a closure in Lua scripting?

2. How are closures different from regular functions in Lua?

3. Explain the concept of encapsulation in relation to closures.

4. How do closures reduce the number of parameters needed in function signatures?

5. In Lua, can closures access variables from their enclosing environment?

6. How can closures be useful in terms of code modularity and reusability?

7. Can closures adapt their behavior based on the conditions present during their creation? Explain.

8. How can closures be assigned to variables and invoked as functions?

Exercises

1. Create a closure named counter that keeps track of a count variable. The closure should have a function increment that increases the count by 1 and a function getCount that returns the current count.

2. Write a closure called calculator that takes two numbers as arguments during its creation. The closure should have functions add and subtract that perform addition and subtraction operations on the given numbers respectively. Test the closure with different values.

3. Implement a closure named listOperations that stores a table of numbers. The closure should have functions addToList to add a number to the list, getLength to retrieve the length of the list, and sumList to calculate the sum of the numbers in the list. Test the closure with various numbers.

4. Create a closure named temperatureConverter that converts temperature from Celsius to Fahrenheit. The closure should have functions toFahrenheit and toCelsius that perform the conversions. Test the closure with different temperature values.

5. Develop a closure called shoppingCart that keeps track of items added to a cart. The closure should have functions addItem to add an item to the cart and getItems to retrieve a list of items in the cart. Test the closure by adding and retrieving various items.

Chapter 12: Operating System Library

In this chapter, we'll dive into the OS (Operating System) library, which provides a range of pre-built tools to retrieve valuable information from the device. The OS library offers various functions that can assist you in understanding time, date, and other operating system-related details.

Learning Objectives

Upon completing this chapter on the Lua OS library, you will be able to:

➢ Understand the purpose of the OS library in Lua and its role in interacting with the operating system.

➢ Employ the os.date() function to format dates and times based on specified patterns.

➢ Execute external commands using os.execute() and handle the resulting success or failure.

➢ Terminate a Lua program using os.exit() and specify the exit status.

➢ Retrieve environment variables using os.getenv() and utilize them in your Lua scripts.

➢ Explore the usage of os.setlocale() to set the locale for the program and consider platform-specific implications.

Clock and os.time:

The `clock` function is incredibly useful when you need to measure the execution time of a specific piece of code. It helps us determine how long it takes for a set of code to execute. Another important function is os.time, which converts a given date and time into seconds. By default, it returns the total number of seconds that have elapsed since January 1, 1970 (also known as the *Unix epoch*). Let's take a look at a couple of examples:

Example: Using os.clock to measure execution time

```
local startTime = os.clock()
    -- Your code here
local endTime = os.clock()
local elapsedTime = endTime - startTime
print("Elapsed time:", elapsedTime)
```

This allows a developer to easily track the time it takes for a program to execute a specific set of instructions or functions, making it easier to determine if a particular piece of code takes too long to execute.

Example: Using os.time to get the current date and time

```
local secondsSinceEpoch = os.time()
print("Seconds since 1970:", secondsSinceEpoch)
```

Our second example provides the number of seconds that have elapsed since the Unix epoch (Jan. 1, 1970).

Working with specific dates
In addition to the current date and time, we can use `os.time` to calculate the number of seconds from a specific date and time. By providing a table with year, month, day, hour, minute, and second values to `os.time`, we can obtain the corresponding seconds since 1970.

Example: Calculating the seconds from a specific date and time

```
local specificDateTime = {year = 1999, month = 1,
day = 1, hour = 12, min = 0, sec = 0}
local secondsSinceTime =
os.time(specificDateTime)
print("Seconds since 1970:", secondsSinceTime)
```

Finding the difference between two dates
By utilizing the os.difftime function, we can calculate the time difference in seconds between two specific dates. This information can be handy if you need to measure the duration between two events.

Example: Calculating the time difference between two dates

```
local t1 = os.time()        -- Current time
```

```
local t2 = os.time({year = 2000, month = 1, day = 1,
hour = 0, min = 0, sec = 0})
local timeDifference = os.difftime(t1, t2)
print("Time difference in seconds:", timeDifference)
– Time elapsed since the beginning of the new
millennium
```

Converting seconds back to date and time
To convert seconds back into a human-readable format, we can utilize the `os.date` function. It takes a time number value as an argument and returns a table containing various date and time components.

Example: Converting seconds back to date and time

```
local currentTime = os.time()
local formattedDate = os.date("%A, %B %d, %Y %X",
currentTime)
print("Formatted date:", formattedDate)
```

In the line of code local formattedDate = os.date("%A, %B %d, %Y %X", currentTime), we are using the os.date function to format a date and time string based on a given timestamp (currentTime). Let's break down the formatting pattern used in the code:

> **%A** - Represents the full weekday name (e.g., "Sunday", "Monday").
> **,** - Represents a comma and space character, used for separating the weekday from the rest of the date.

- ➢ **%B** - Represents the full month name (e.g., "January", "February").
- ➢ **%d** - Represents the day of the month as a two-digit number (e.g., "01", "02", ..., "31").
- ➢ **%Y**: Represents the four-digit year (e.g., "2023").
- ➢ **%X**: Represents the time in the format "HH:MM:SS" using the current locale (the current time on the computer on which the program was run).

By combining these format specifiers and characters, we create a pattern that represents the desired date and time format. In this case, the pattern %A, %B %d, %Y %X will produce a formatted date and time string in the following format: "Weekday, Month Day, Year Time".

For example, the output might be "Thursday, June 29, 2023 14:30:45" depending on the current timestamp. Feel free to modify the format string ("%A, %B %d, %Y %X") to suit your specific formatting requirements.

Exploring additional parameters
The os.date function allows us to extract specific information from the returned table. For example, we can obtain the day of the week, year, month, and more.

Example: Working with os.date

```
local currentTimestamp = os.time() -- Get the
```

```
current timestamp
local formattedDate = os.date("%A, %B %d, %Y",
currentTimestamp) -- Format the date
print("Current Date:", formattedDate)
```

In this example, we first use the os.time() function to obtain the current timestamp. The os.time() function returns the number of seconds that have elapsed since January 1st, 1970.

Next, we use os.date to format the date using the obtained timestamp. The os.date function takes two arguments: the format string and the timestamp. The format string specifies the desired format for the date string. In this case, "%A, %B %d, %Y" represents the format we want to use, just like above.

After formatting the date, we store it in the formattedDate variable. Finally, we print the formatted date to the console using print.

When you run this code, it will display the current date in the specified format. For example, the output might be: "Current Date: Thursday, June 29, 2023".

Executing Commands with os.execute

The os.execute function allows us to execute commands through the operating system's shell. It behaves similarly to the ISO C function system. When a command is provided, os.execute returns true if the command terminated successfully. If the command fails, it returns fail. Additionally, os.execute can return a string and a number with additional information about the command execution:

- ➤ If the command terminated normally, the string returned is "exit", and the number represents the exit status of the command.
- ➤ If the command was terminated by a signal, the string returned is "signal", and the number represents the signal that terminated the command.
- ➤ If os.execute is called without a command, it returns a boolean indicating whether a shell is available.

Example: Executing a command using os.execute

```
local command = "ls"  – Mac OS or Linux - lists files
in current folder
– local command = "dir" - Windows - lists files in
current folder
local success = os.execute(command)

if success then
    print("Command executed successfully!")
else
    print("Command failed to execute.")
end
```

Exiting the Program with os.exit:

The os.exit function terminates the Lua program and calls the ISO C function exit behind the scenes. It accepts an optional code parameter that determines the exit status of the program. The behavior of os.exit depends on the value of code:

If code is true, the returned status is EXIT_SUCCESS.

If code is false, the returned status is EXIT_FAILURE.

If code is a number, the returned status is the provided number.

By default, if no code is specified, the returned status is EXIT_SUCCESS. Additionally, you can include an optional second argument, close, which, if set to true, will close the Lua state before exiting. Here's an example:

Example: Exiting the program with os.exit

```
local exitStatus = true
os.exit(exitStatus)
```

Retrieving Environment Variables with os.getenv

The os.getenv function allows us to retrieve the value of a specific process environment variable that you specified. It returns the value of the variable if it is defined. If the variable is not defined, os.getenv returns fail.

Example: Retrieving an environment variable with os.getenv

```
local username = os.getenv("OS")
if username then
    print("Operating System:", username)
else
    print("Operating System variable not defined.")
end
```

Here are some common parameters that can be used with os.getenv():

- ➤ **"HOME"** - Returns the path to the user's home directory.
- ➤ **"USER"** - Returns the username of the currently logged-in user.
- ➤ **"PATH"** - Returns the system's search path for executables.
- ➤ **"TEMP"** or **"TMP"** - Returns the path to the temporary directory.
- ➤ **"OS"** - Returns the name of the operating system.
- ➤ **"LANG"** - Returns the current locale or language setting.
- ➤ **"PWD"** - Returns the current working directory.
- ➤ **"SHELL"** - Returns the path to the default shell or command interpreter.
- ➤ **"DISPLAY"** - Returns the display name or address for graphical applications (Mac/Linux/Unix systems).
- ➤ **"APPDATA"** - Returns the path to the application data directory (Windows systems).

Removing Files with os.remove

The os.remove function deletes a file (or an empty directory on some Unix-based systems) with the provided filename. If the deletion fails, os.remove returns fail along with a string describing the error and the error code. On success, it returns true.

Example: Removing a file with os.remove

```
local filename = "myfile.txt"
local success, errorMessage = os.remove(filename)
if success then
    print("File removed successfully.")
else
    print("Failed to remove file:", errorMessage)
end
```

Renaming Files or Directories with os.rename

The os.rename function allows us to rename a file or directory from oldname to newname. If the renaming operation fails, os.rename returns fail along with a string describing the error and the error code. On success, it returns true. Let's look at an example:

Example: Renaming a file or directory with os.rename

```
local oldname = "myfile.txt"
local newname = "newfile.txt"
local success, errorMessage = os.rename(oldname,
newname)
```

```
if success then
    print("Renaming successful.")
else
    print("Failed to rename:", errorMessage)
end
```

Setting the Locale with os.setlocale

The os.setlocale function allows us to set the locale (language and cultural preferences) for the program. It takes a locale parameter as the desired locale string and an optional category parameter specifying the category to modify. However, the detailed usage and behavior of os.setlocale can vary across different Lua implementations and platforms. Consult the Lua documentation or platform-specific resources for more information on using this function effectively (https://www.lua.org/manual/5.4/manual.html#pdf-os.setlocale).

Example: Setting the locale with os.setlocale

```
-- Set the locale to United States English
os.setlocale("en_US.UTF-8")
```

Conclusion

You've learned about several useful functions provided by the OS library in Lua. These functions empower you to execute commands, exit the program, work with environment variables, manage files and directories, and manipulate locales. Remember to explore the Lua documentation for more details on each function and experiment with different use cases.

Questions

1. What is the purpose of the OS library in Lua?

2. How can you format dates and times using the os.date() function?

3. What does the os.execute() function do?

4. How can you handle the success or failure of an executed command using os.execute()?

5. How does os.exit() terminate a Lua program?

6. What does the os.getenv() function retrieve?

7. How does the clock function help measure execution time in Lua?

8. How do you find the time difference between two specific dates using os.difftime()?

9. How can you convert seconds back into a human-readable date and time format using os.date()?

10. How do you remove a file using the os.remove() function in Lua?

Exercises

1. Write a Lua program that uses os.date() to print the current date and time in a specific format.

2. Create a Lua script that executes a command of your choice using os.execute().

3. Write a Lua program that measures the execution time of a specific code block using os.clock().

4. Create a Lua script that calculates the number of seconds between two specific dates and prints the result.

5. Write a Lua script that retrieves the operating system name using os.getenv() and displays it to the console.

Chapter 13: Modules

In this chapter, we will explore the fascinating world of modules in Lua. Modules are powerful tools that allow you to create your own libraries of useful subroutines or functions. They enable you to organize your code more effectively, reuse common functionality, and make your programs more modular and maintainable.

Learning Objectives

➤ Understand the concept of modules in Lua.

➤ Explain the purpose of modules as containers for functions, variables, and Lua code.

➤ Use the require command to include modules in your Lua applications.

➤ Differentiate between storing the module table in a variable and directly accessing module functions.

➤ Create a simple module in Lua with functions and variables.

Understanding Modules

Modules in Lua serve as containers for functions, variables, and other Lua code. They are like self-contained libraries that can be easily included in your applications using a single command: require. When you require a module, it returns a table containing all the functionality defined in that module. This table can then be used within your program to access the functions and variables provided by the module. To better understand the functionality of modules, let's create a simple module.

Creating a Simple Module

To illustrate how modules work, let's create a simple module called my_module.lua. This module will contain two functions: *add* and *hi*:

```
--my_module.lua
local sample = {}

function sample.add(a, b)
    return a + b
end

function sample.hi(letter)
    return "hi " .. letter
end

return sample
```

In this module, we define a table called sample, and within it, we have two functions: *add* and *hi*. By using the period after the table name (sample), we have added the functions to the sample table. The add function takes two numbers as arguments and returns their sum. The hi function takes a letter as an argument and returns a greeting message.

Note that both functions, add and hi, are stored in the sample table. When sample is returned at the end of the module, which is saved to its own file in the same folder as the function Lua program that will call it, we have all of the functions in my_module.lua available to other Lua programs.

There are two ways to include a module in Lua: using a variable to store the module table or directly accessing the module functions.

Storing the Module Table

The first approach is to set up a variable that will hold the module table. Let's name our variable my_mod and assign it the value returned by require for our module.

```
local my_mod = require("my_module")

print(my_mod.hi("A"))    -- Output: hi A
print(my_mod.add(1, 5)) -- Output: 6
```

In this example, we load my_module into memory of our calling program by using require and store its table in the my_mod variable. We can then access the functions in the module using dot notation (my_mod.function_name).

Directly Accessing Module Functions

Alternatively, if you don't need to store the module table in a variable, you can directly access the module functions using the module name and dot notation. Here's an example:

```
require("my_module")

print(sample.hi("B"))    -- Output: hi B
print(sample.add(2, 4)) -- Output: 6
```

In this example, we directly call the functions from the module using the table name (sample) and dot notation. Notice that we did not need to assign the require result to a variable. However, it's important to note that this approach assumes that the module table has the same name as the module itself. In general, most programmers prefer to store the module in a variable to ensure that they have access to the resources in the module.

Exploring the Power of Modules

Modules provide an incredibly powerful feature in Lua, allowing us to simulate many capabilities of object-oriented programming. Although Lua is not an object-oriented language, using tables and modules in this way can provide similar benefits.

By encapsulating related functions and variables within a module, we can create reusable and modular code. We can organize our code logically, improve code maintenance, and make our programs more efficient.

Modules can include functions and variables that are not directly available to other developers, which allows the programmer to create routines that solve complex problems without exposing them to the outside world. This 'black-box' approach to programming is very similar to the approach used in object-oriented languages.

Finding Existing Modules

A wide variety of Lua modules, known as packages, are available on the internet. These packages are pre-written modules created by others to help speed up your programming. You can find them on various websites or repositories dedicated to Lua programming. These packages cover various areas such as game development, networking, graphics, and more. We will further discuss some of these modules in a later chapter when we cover Lua Rocks.

Conclusion

In this chapter, we have explored the concept of modules in Lua. We learned that modules allow us to create our own libraries of functions and variables, making our code more modular and reusable. We saw how to create a simple module and how to include it in our applications using the require command. We also discovered the power of modules in providing organized and efficient code.

Questions

1. What is the purpose of modules in Lua?

2. How can modules be included in Lua applications?

3. What is the role of the require command in using modules?

4. How does a module return its functionality to the calling program?

5. What is the advantage of storing the module table in a variable?

6. How can you directly access module functions without storing the module table?

7. Explain the process of creating a simple module in Lua.

8. What are the benefits of using modules for code organization and reusability?

9. How do modules in Lua simulate object-oriented programming?

Exercises

1. Create a module called "math_functions.lua" that includes functions for calculating the area and perimeter of a rectangle.

2. Write a Lua program that uses a module to calculate the area and perimeter of a rectangle with length 5 and width 8.

3. Design a module called "temperature_conversion.lua" that includes functions for converting Celsius to Fahrenheit and vice versa.

Chapter 14: Recursion

In this chapter, we will dive into the exciting world of recursion in Lua scripting. Recursion is a powerful concept that involves a function calling itself, allowing us to solve complex problems and create fascinating programming solutions. In this chapter, we will explore the basics of recursion, understand its importance, and learn how to implement recursive functions in Lua. We will also discuss the importance of defining an exit condition to avoid infinite loops. So, let's get started and unleash the power of recursion!

Learning Objectives

➢ Understand the concept of recursion in computer programming and scripting.

➢ Identify the benefits and applications of using recursion in problem-solving.

➢ Define and explain the base case or exit condition in recursive functions.

➢ Recognize the importance of making progress towards the base case to avoid infinite recursion.

➢ Implement recursive functions in Lua and understand the flow of execution.

➢ Control the depth of recursion by introducing additional parameters.

➢ Solve the Tower of Hanoi problem using recursion and understand its rules and constraints.

➢ Generate the Fibonacci sequence using recursive algorithms.

Understanding Recursion

Recursion is a fundamental concept in computer programming and scripting. It involves a function calling itself during its execution. This recursive process continues until a specific condition, known as the base case or exit condition, is met. Recursion provides an elegant way to solve complex problems by breaking them down into smaller, more manageable subproblems.

Why Use Recursion?

Recursion is widely used in programming for various reasons:

➢ It allows us to solve problems that have a repetitive or recursive nature, such as finding the factorial of a number or searching through a binary tree.
➢ It simplifies code by reducing complex problems into smaller, more understandable parts.

> It can be used to create fascinating visual effects, such as generating fractals or animating recursive patterns.

Guidelines for Using Recursion

When using recursion, it's crucial to follow a few guidelines to ensure its proper functioning:

> Define an exit condition: Every recursive function must have an exit condition (also known as a 'base case') that terminates the recursion. Without an exit condition, the function will result in an infinite loop, consuming system resources and eventually causing a stack overflow error.
> Ensure progress towards the base case. Otherwise, the recursion will continue indefinitely, leading to stack overflow errors.
> Break down the problem: Recursion works by breaking down a problem into smaller subproblems. Each recursive call should handle a smaller instance of the problem until it reaches the base case.

Implementing Recursion

Let's dive into an example to understand how recursion works in Lua. Consider the following code snippet:

```lua
function recursive( counter )
        counter = counter + 1
        print( "I'm recurring " .. counter )
```

```
        if counter < 5 then
            recursive( counter )
        end
        print( "Too late, I recurred, already! I was
recursion " .. counter )
end

recursive( 0 )
```

Output
I'm recurring 1
I'm recurring 2
I'm recurring 3
I'm recurring 4
I'm recurring 5
Too late, I recurred, already! I was recursion 5
Too late, I recurred, already! I was recursion 4
Too late, I recurred, already! I was recursion 3
Too late, I recurred, already! I was recursion 2
Too late, I recurred, already! I was recursion 1

In this example, the recursive function is called with an initial counter value of 0. The function checks if the counter is less than 5. If it is, the function calls itself with the updated counter value (counter + 1). This recursive call continues until the counter reaches 5, at which point the recursion stops.

The power of recursion lies in its ability to perform actions after the recursive call. In this case, the print statement executes only after the recursive call has completed (i.e., the value of counter is < 5). This ensures that the function counts up to 5 before displaying the counter values. Once the exit condition or base case is met, the function returns control to the calling function, then we have an output that counts down from the exit condition.

Recursive Control

Sometimes, it is necessary to control the depth of recursion to prevent excessive resource consumption. We can achieve this by introducing an additional parameter, such as a limit, to control the recursion depth.

```
function recursive(counter, limit)
    if counter < limit then
        recursive(counter + 1, limit)
    end
    print("Current counter:", counter)
end

recursive(1, 6)
```

Output
```
Current counter:    6
Current counter:    5
Current counter:    4
Current counter:    3
Current counter:    2
Current counter:    1
```

In this example, the recursive function now takes an additional parameter, limit, which determines the maximum recursion depth. By passing the desired limit to the function, we can control the number of recursive calls made.

Practical Applications of Recursion

Recursion finds practical applications in various programming projects, especially in introductory programming classes. Here are a few examples.

Tower of Hanoi

The Tower of Hanoi is a classic puzzle that involves moving a stack of disks from one peg to another, following specific rules. According to popular legend, there was a temple in the Indian city of Benares (now Varanasi) with three diamond needles. The priests at the temple were responsible for moving 64 golden disks of various sizes from one needle to another, following the rules of the puzzle.

The priests believed that once they completed the task, the world would come to an end. Hence, they kept moving the disks, passing the responsibility from generation to generation. Perhaps they are not very motivated to complete the task?

The puzzle consists of three pegs, usually labeled A, B, and C, and a set of disks of different sizes.

The rules for the Tower of Hanoi problem are as follows:

> Only one disk can be moved at a time: At each step, you can only move the top disk from one peg to another or place it on an empty peg.
> Larger disks cannot be placed on top of smaller disks: A larger disk must always be placed below a smaller disk. This rule ensures that the tower remains stable throughout the process.
> All disks must be moved from the source peg to the destination peg: The goal is to transfer the entire stack of disks from the source peg to the destination peg using the auxiliary peg as a temporary holding area.

Let's see how we can solve this puzzle using recursion in Lua.

To solve the Tower of Hanoi problem, you follow a recursive algorithm:

1. Define the base case: If there is only one disk to move, simply move it from the source peg to the destination peg.
2. Recursive step: For any number of disks greater than one, follow these steps:
    a. Move the top n-1 disks from the source peg to the auxiliary peg, using the destination peg as the temporary peg.
    b. Move the largest disk from the source peg to the destination peg.
    c. Move the n-1 disks from the auxiliary peg to the destination peg, using the source peg as the temporary peg.

By applying these rules recursively, the Tower of Hanoi problem can be solved efficiently. The minimum number of moves required to solve the problem with n disks is 2^n - 1.

```
function towerOfHanoi(n, source, destination,
auxiliary)
   if n > 0 then
      -- Move n-1 disks from the source peg to the
auxiliary peg
      towerOfHanoi(n - 1, source, auxiliary,
destination)

      -- Move the nth disk from the source peg to the
destination peg
      print("Move disk", n, "from", source, "to",
destination)

      -- Move the n-1 disks from the auxiliary peg to
the destination peg
      towerOfHanoi(n - 1, auxiliary, destination,
source)
   end
end

-- Usage: towerOfHanoi(num_disks, 'source',
'destination', 'auxiliary')
towerOfHanoi(3, 'A', 'C', 'B')

Output
Move disk    1    from  A    to    C
Move disk    2    from  A    to    B
Move disk    1    from  C    to    B
Move disk    3    from  A    to    C
```

```
Move disk    1    from  B    to    A
Move disk    2    from  B    to    C
Move disk    1    from  A    to    C
```

By running this code, you will see the sequence of moves required to solve the Tower of Hanoi puzzle with 3 disks.

Fibonacci Sequence

The Fibonacci sequence is a series of numbers in which each number is the sum of the two preceding ones. The first two numbers are always 1. Then, to find the next number, you just add the last two numbers together. So, 1 + 1 = 2, and 1 + 2 = 3, and 2 + 3 = 5, and so on, resulting in a series of numbers like this: 1, 1, 2, 3, 5, 8, 13, and so on.

The sequence keeps going forever, and each number is like a little puzzle piece that fits perfectly with the others.

The Fibonacci sequence appears all around us in nature, like in flower petals, pinecones, and even in the number of spirals in a seashell. It's like a secret code that nature uses to make beautiful patterns.

Recursion provides an elegant way to generate the Fibonacci sequence.

```
function fibonacci(n)
```

```
   if n <= 1 then
      return n
   else
      return fibonacci(n - 1) + fibonacci(n - 2)
   end
end

-- Usage: print(fibonacci(n))
print(fibonacci(6))
```

Output
8

In this example, the fibonacci function recursively calculates the nth Fibonacci number. If n is less than or equal to 1, it directly returns n. Otherwise, it makes recursive calls to calculate the (n-1)th and (n-2)th Fibonacci numbers and adds them together to obtain the nth Fibonacci number.

By running this code, you will see the 6th Fibonacci number being computed, which is 8.

Conclusion

Recursion is a powerful concept in Lua scripting that allows us to solve complex problems and create fascinating programming solutions. By understanding the basics of recursion, following guidelines for implementation, and defining appropriate exit conditions, you can harness its full potential. The Tower of Hanoi problem and the Fibonacci sequence are just a couple of examples demonstrating the practical applications of recursion.

Questions

1. What is recursion, and why is it a fundamental concept in computer programming?

2. How does recursion simplify code and help solve complex problems?

3. What is the base case or exit condition, and why is it necessary in recursive functions?

4. What happens if a recursive function does not have an exit condition?

5. Explain the flow of execution in a recursive function.

6. How can you control the depth of recursion to prevent excessive resource consumption?

7. How does recursion help solve the Tower of Hanoi problem?

8. What is the Fibonacci sequence, and how can recursion be used to generate it?

9. Explain the recursive algorithm for generating the Fibonacci sequence.

Exercises

1. Write a recursive function to calculate the factorial of a given number.

2. Create a recursive function to calculate the power of a number given the base and exponent.

3. Write a Lua program to recursively reverse a string.

4. Implement a recursive function to check if a given string is a palindrome.

Part III: Advanced Lua Concepts

Chapter 15: Objects in Lua

In this chapter, we will explore the concept of simulating programming objects using Lua. Object-oriented programming (OOP) is a popular paradigm in software development, and while Lua is not a true object-oriented programming language, it provides us with powerful tools to simulate object-like structures using tables. We will learn how to use tables to store values and functions, and how to leverage Lua's metamethods and meta tables to create object-oriented simulations. By the end of this chapter, you will have a solid understanding of how to create and manipulate objects in Lua.

Learning Objectives

> Understand the concept of object-oriented programming and how it organizes code around objects.

> Explore Lua's approach to creating objects using tables.

> Learn how to assign and modify objects in Lua.

> Understand how to invoke object methods in Lua.

> Use methods to create dynamic and interactive objects.

> Understand the importance of encapsulation and how to achieve it using modules in Lua.

➢ Explore the concept of metatables and metamethods in Lua.

➢ Learn how to modify table behavior using metatables and metamethods.

➢ Explore common metamethods and their usage in Lua.

Understanding Objects in Lua

Before we dive into simulating objects in Lua, let's discuss what object-oriented programming is. Object-oriented programming is a programming paradigm that organizes code around objects, which are instances of classes. Objects encapsulate data (attributes) and behavior (methods) related to a specific concept or entity. Objects can interact with each other by invoking methods or accessing attributes.

While Lua does not have built-in support for classes, we can use Lua's table data structure to create objects. Tables in Lua can store values and functions, making them suitable for creating object-like structures. Although Lua's approach to objects differs from traditional object-oriented programming, it provides us with flexibility and control over our code.

Creating an Object with Tables

Previously in Chapter 9, we discussed using tables in the form of creating key-value structures. This is the heart of using Lua to create objects. You might something similar from that chapter:

```
-- Creating a pet object
pet = {
  type = "",
  message = "hungry",
  hungry = function(self)
      print("The pet is hungry!")
  end,
  points = 0
}
```

In this code snippet, we define a table called **pet**. Inside this table, we have various **keys** such as **type**, **message**, **hungry**, and **points**. These keys represent the attributes of our pet object. The **type** key is initially an empty string, the **message** key is set to "hungry," and **points** is initialized to 0. The **hungry** key is assigned a **closure** function (see chapter 9 for a refresher in closures) that prints a message to the screen. This function represents a behavior or method of our pet object.

Assigning and Modifying Objects

To create an object from our table, we can assign it to a variable. Let's assign the pet table to a variable named dog:

```
-- Assigning the pet object to the dog variable
local dog = pet
```

By assigning pet to dog, we create a reference to the same table. Any modifications made to dog will also affect the original pet table. In Lua, tables are passed by reference, meaning that both dog and pet point to the same underlying data structure.

Here is an example:

```lua
local pet = {
    type = "",
    message = "hungry",
    hungry = function(self)
        print("The pet is hungry!")
    end,
    points = 0
}

local dog = pet

pet.type = "cat"

print(dog.type)
```

Output
cat

Invoking Object Methods

In object-oriented programming, objects can perform actions or behaviors through methods. To invoke a method on our object, we can use the colon operator (:). The colon operator allows us to pass the object itself as an argument to the method. Let's call the hungry method on our dog object:

```
-- Calling the hungry method on the dog object
dog:hungry()

Output
The pet is hungry!
```

The hungry method receives the object itself as an argument, which we refer to as self inside the method. By using the colon operator, we pass dog as self to the hungry function. This allows the method to access and manipulate the attributes of the object.

Using Methods to Create Objects

Methods play a crucial role in object-oriented programming as they encapsulate the behavior of objects. In Lua, we can utilize methods to enhance the creation and manipulation of objects. Let's extend our pet object example to include a method that allows us to change the pet's type:

```lua
local pet = {
    type = "",
    message = "hungry",
    hungry = function(self)
        print("The pet is hungry!")
    end,
    points = 0
}
```

```
-- Adding a method to change the pet's type
pet.changeType = function(self, newType)
   self.type = newType
end

local dog = pet

dog:changeType("dog")
print(dog.type)
```

Output
dog

In the code above, we define a new method called changeType for our pet object. This method takes two arguments: self and newType. The self parameter represents the object (pet), and newType is the new type of pet we want to assign to the pet. Inside the method, we update the type attribute of the object using self.type = newType. This allows us to modify the object's type dynamically.

By calling the changeType method on the dog object and passing "dog" as the new type, we effectively modify the type attribute of the dog object. Subsequently, printing dog.type displays the updated type, "dog"

Using methods in Lua gives us the ability to define specific behaviors for our objects, making them more dynamic and interactive.

Designing Objects

As stated previously, objects are simply tables that contain values and functions. The idea is that the functions contained in the object can, and often do, manipulate the values within the same object. As these objects map to real paradigms, they will normally facilitate a specific group of tasks. For example, should I want to develop a game about a dog, I might need a dog object. This object may have methods that allow the dog to bark, run, or wag its tail, while the dog's properties might describe the direction the dog is running, whether its tail is currently wagging, and what the dog might say when it barks. The following is a simple object that shows this example in action:

```
directions = { north = "northerly", east = "easterly",
south = "southerly", west =
        "westerly" }
dog = {}
dog.barkMessage = "I'm hungry. Feed me!"
dog.direction = directions.north
dog.isWagging = false
dog.bark = function()
    print( dog.barkMessage )
end

dog.doWag = function()
    dog.isWagging = true
end

dog.stopWag = function()
```

```
    dog.isWagging = false
end

dog.run = function()
    print ( "Dog is running in the " .. dog.direction .. "
direction" )
end

dog.bark()
```
Output   I'm hungry. Feed me!

```
dog.doWag()
print ( dog.isWagging )
```
Output   true

```
dog.stopWag()
print ( dog.isWagging )
```
Output   false

```
dog.run()
```
Output   Dog is running in the northerly direction

```
dog.direction = directions.south
dog.run()
```
Output   Dog is running in the southerly direction

This is a start, but there are lots of inefficiencies here. To begin with, objects are supposed to be self-contained (or 'encapsulated'). However, here, in order to access values of the dog object within the object's methods, we need to relate specifically to the dog object. This is poor practice and could lead to problems further down the line. For example, what happens when we want to create more than one of these objects? We can't have all instances of this object accessing the same data.

Encapsulation and Modules

Encapsulation is a fundamental concept in object-oriented programming that refers to the bundling of data and methods together within an object, providing data hiding and abstraction. Lua allows us to achieve encapsulation through the use of modules. See chapter 13 for a discussion on how to create a module.

A module in Lua is a way to organize and encapsulate related code. It provides a mechanism for creating reusable components and achieving information hiding. Let's see how we can use modules to encapsulate our pet object.

pet.lua

```lua
-- Creating a pet module
local pet = {}

function pet.new()
    local obj = {
        type = "",
        message = "hungry",
        points = 0
    }

    function obj:hungry()
        print("The pet is hungry!")
```

```
   end

     return obj
 end

 return pet
```

In this code snippet, we define a module called pet. Inside the module, we have a new function that creates and returns a new instance of the pet object. The new function initializes the pet's attributes and methods. Note the use of local to create local variables within the module, ensuring encapsulation.

To use the pet module and create pet objects, we can import it into our main Lua script:

main.lua

```
local pet = require("pet")

-- Creating a pet object
local dog = pet.new()

-- Modifying the dog object
dog.type = "dog"
dog:hungry()

Output
The pet is hungry!
```

By utilizing modules, we encapsulate the implementation details of our pet object, exposing only the necessary interface. Other parts of our program can import the module and create pet objects without directly accessing or modifying the internal structure of the object. In other words, if we create a second pet named cat and change its type, we will not impact the original dog object.

Note: *it is required to place the pet module in its own file. Best practices require that you name the file the same as the module name (i.e. pet.lua).*

Encapsulation allows for better code organization, information hiding, and modularity, leading to more maintainable and reusable code.

Metatables and Metamethods
Metatables and metamethods allow us to redefine how operations are performed on tables in Lua. By the end of this section, you will understand how to use metatables and metamethods to customize table behavior and enable advanced programming techniques.

Introduction to Metatables and Metamethods
In Lua, metatables are special tables that define the behavior of other tables. They allow us to override and customize operations such as addition, subtraction, comparison, and more. Metamethods, on the other hand, are functions associated with metatables that handle these operations. By using metatables and metamethods, we can create powerful abstractions

and extend Lua's capabilities.

Modifying Addition with Metatables

Let's begin by considering a simple example. Suppose we have two tables, table1 and table2, each with a key-value set to 100 and 200, respectively. If we try to add these tables together using the + operator, Lua will throw an error because it doesn't know how to handle table addition.

To address this, we can define a metamethod for addition, specifically the __add metamethod. This metamethod will be invoked whenever the + operator is used on a table.

Let's take a look at an example:

```lua
-- Define the metamethod
local myMetaMethod_add = function(a, b)
    return { value = a.value + b.value }
end

-- Create a metatable and associate the
metamethod with it
local addTables= {
  __add = myMetaMethod_add
}

local table1 = { value = 100 }
local table2 = { value = 200 }

-- Set the metatable for table1
setmetatable(table1, addTables)
```

```
-- Perform the addition
local result = table1 + table2
print("Result:", result.value)
```

Output
Result: 300

In this example, we create a metamethod named **myMetaMethod_add** that takes two tables (a and b) as arguments and returns a new table with the summed values in the key 'value'. We then define a metatable (addTables) and associate the __add metamethod with our custom function. Finally, we use setmetatable command to set addTables as the metatable for table1.

When we perform the addition operation (table1 + table2), Lua will automatically invoke our metamethod, resulting in a new table with the summed values.

Matrix Addition with Metamethods
Now, let's explore a more advanced use case of metatables and metamethods: matrix addition. Matrix addition involves adding corresponding elements of two matrices together. Although it is not a built-in feature of Lua, we can create a metamethod to handle matrix addition for tables.

If we have two matrices (table1 and table2)

table1 =

$$\begin{bmatrix} 1 & 2 & 3 \\ 4 & 5 & 6 \\ 7 & 8 & 9 \end{bmatrix}$$

table2 =

$$\begin{bmatrix} 10 & 11 & 12 \\ 13 & 14 & 15 \\ 16 & 17 & 18 \end{bmatrix}$$

Here's an example of how to perform matrix addition using metatables and metamethods:

```
-- Define the matrix addition function
local matrix_add = function(a, b)
    local rows = #a
    local columns = #a[1]
    local result = {}

    for i = 1, rows do
        result[i] = {}
        for j = 1, columns do
            result[i][j] = a[i][j] + b[i][j]
```

```
        end
    end

    return result
end

-- Create a metatable and associate the matrix_add
function with it
local matrixAddTable = {
    __add = matrix_add
}

local table1 = {{1, 2, 3}, {4, 5, 6}, {7, 8, 9}}
local table2 = {{10, 11, 12}, {13, 14, 15}, {16, 17, 18}}

-- Set the metatable for table1
setmetatable(table1, matrixAddTable)

-- Perform matrix addition
local result = table1 + table2
    print("Result:")
    for i = 1, #result do
        for j = 1, #result[1] do
            io.write(result[i][j], " ")
        end
        io.write("\n")
    end
```

Output
```
Result:
11 13 15
17 19 21
23 25 27
```

In this example, we define the matrix_add function that takes two tables (table1 and table2) representing matrices and returns a new table with the corresponding elements added together. We then create a metatable (matrixAddTable) and associate the __add metamethod with our matrix_add function.

When we perform the matrix addition (table1 + table2), the metamethod matrix_add will be called automatically, resulting in a new table containing the summed values.

Common Metamethods and their Usage

There are a number of common metamethods. Here are some of the most common.

Note: *all of the following metamethods are preceded by two underscore key strokes. In some printing or ebook conversions, this may appear to be a single long underscore.*

__index Metamethod

The __index metamethod is a feature in Lua that allows us to customize table behavior when indexing or accessing values. Its purpose is to retrieve values from tables and handle cases when keys are not found.

With the __index metamethod, we can define a function or a table to be associated with a metatable. When a key is not found in a table, Lua automatically calls this metamethod to determine the value to return. This enables us to create dynamic and flexible table structures.

By implementing the __index metamethod, we can customize the behavior of table indexing and provide default values or perform additional operations. For example, if a key is not present in a table, we can choose to return a default value instead of producing an error. This ensures smoother program execution and better error handling.

__newindex Metamethod

The __newindex metamethod in Lua allows us to modify the behavior of table assignments and handle cases when keys are not found. Its purpose is to customize how tables are updated or modified when new values are assigned to them.

By implementing the __newindex metamethod, we can define a function or a table to be associated with a metatable. When a key is assigned a value in a table, Lua automatically calls this metamethod to determine how to handle the assignment. This gives us control over how values are updated and allows for advanced manipulation of table data.

The __newindex metamethod is particularly useful when we want to enforce restrictions, perform validations, or trigger specific actions when modifying table values. It provides a way to intercept assignments and customize the behavior according to our needs.

__add and __sub Metamethods

The __add and __sub metamethods in Lua provide a way to customize the behavior of addition and subtraction operations for tables. These metamethods allow us to define how tables should behave when they are added or subtracted together, giving us greater flexibility and control over these operations. We have already seen one example of how to use the __add metamethod. The __sub metamethod works in the same fashion.

The purpose of the __add metamethod is to define the behavior of the addition operation when performed on tables. By associating a function with the __add metamethod, we can specify how table addition should be handled. Similarly, the __sub metamethod allows us to customize the subtraction operation for tables.

With the __add and __sub metamethods, we can handle scenarios such as:

> ➢ Combining table data: We can define how tables should be merged or combined when using the addition operation. This can be useful when working with complex data structures or when combining data from multiple sources.

> ➢ Performing mathematical operations: By associating a function with the __add or __sub metamethod, we can perform mathematical calculations on table values. This allows us to create powerful algorithms or perform computations involving table data.

__mul and __div Metamethods

The __mul and __div metamethods in Lua serve the purpose of customizing the behavior of multiplication and division operations for tables, just like the __add metamethod. These metamethods provide a way to define how tables should interact and behave when multiplied or divided, granting programmers greater control and flexibility over these operations.

The __mul metamethod is used to specify the behavior of the multiplication operation when performed on tables. By associating a function with the __mul metamethod, we can define how table multiplication should be handled. Similarly, the __div metamethod allows us to customize the division operation for tables.

The __mul and __div metamethods offer several practical applications, including:

> ➢ Scaling and transformation: Tables representing geometric objects or coordinates can be multiplied by a scalar value to scale or transform them. For example, multiplying a table representing a vector by a scalar can

increase its magnitude or resize an object in a graphical application.

➢ Matrix operations: Tables can be treated as matrices, and the __mul metamethod can be used to define matrix multiplication. This is particularly useful in scientific and mathematical computations involving matrices, such as linear transformations or solving systems of linear equations.

➢ Proportional calculations: The __mul and __div metamethods can be utilized to perform proportional calculations. For instance, when working with tables representing quantities or measurements, multiplying or dividing them can help determine ratios, proportions, or adjust values accordingly.

➢ Custom data types: By defining the __mul and __div metamethods for custom data types, developers can create objects or structures that support multiplication and division operations tailored to the specific requirements of their programs. This can enable the creation of domain-specific calculations and behaviors.

__eq, __lt, and __le Metamethods

The __eq, __lt, and __le metamethods in Lua serve the purpose of customizing the behavior of equality, less than, and less than or equal to comparisons for tables. These metamethods provide a way to define how tables should be compared and evaluated in terms of their equality and order.

The __eq metamethod is used to specify the behavior of the equality comparison (==) between tables. By associating a function with the __eq metamethod, we can define the criteria for considering two tables as equal. This allows us to compare tables based on specific attributes or properties rather than their memory addresses.

The __lt metamethod is used to define the behavior of the less than comparison (<) between tables. It allows us to determine the order of tables based on a specific criterion. By associating a function with the __lt metamethod, we can define the comparison logic to establish which table should be considered smaller or precede another in a sorted sequence.

The __le metamethod is used to define the behavior of the less than or equal to comparison (<=) between tables. It allows us to determine if one table is less than or equal to another. By associating a function with the __le metamethod, we can establish the conditions under which one table is considered smaller or equal to another.

The __eq, __lt, and __le metamethods offer several practical applications, including:

> Customized sorting: By defining the __lt metamethod, tables can be sorted based on specific attributes or criteria. This enables the creation of custom sorting algorithms that sort

tables in a non-standard order, such as sorting a table of objects based on their properties or attributes.

➢ Unique table identification: The __eq metamethod allows us to define what constitutes equality between tables. This can be useful when working with complex data structures or custom data types that need to be uniquely identified or compared.

➢ Set operations: The __eq, __lt, and __le metamethods can be used to define set operations on tables. For example, by implementing these metamethods, tables can be compared for equality, checked for inclusion in a set, or ordered to perform set operations like union, intersection, or difference.

➢ Object-oriented programming: By defining the __eq metamethod, tables can be used to represent objects, and their equality can be based on specific object attributes or properties. This facilitates object comparison and enables the use of object-oriented programming concepts within Lua.

Modifying Unary Operators

In Lua, it is possible to customize the behavior of unary operators, such as negation (-) and length calculation (#), using metamethods. Metamethods provide a way to define how tables should respond to these unary operations, allowing for the customization of their behavior.

The negation unary operator (-) is used to perform arithmetic negation, changing the sign of a numeric value. By associating a function with the __unm metamethod, tables can be customized to respond to the negation operation. This enables the ability to define specific behaviors when negating a table, such as negating each element of a table or applying a custom mathematical operation to the table's data.

The length calculation unary operator (#) is used to determine the length of a table or the number of elements it contains. By associating a function with the __len metamethod, tables can be customized to provide a custom length calculation. This allows for the implementation of alternative length calculations, such as considering only certain elements or taking into account additional factors.

Customizing unary operations with metamethods offers several practical applications, including:

> Mathematical transformations: The __unm metamethod can be used to perform custom mathematical transformations on tables. For example, a table representing vectors could be negated to calculate the opposite direction or apply specific mathematical operations to each element.

> Alternative length calculations: The __len metamethod enables the customization of how table length is determined. This can be useful when dealing with tables that have a specific structure or when additional factors need to be

considered in the length calculation, such as excluding certain elements or taking into account additional properties.

➢ Complex data structures: Customizing unary operations allows for the creation of complex data structures that respond to negation or length calculation in a specific way. This enables the development of data structures tailored to specific application requirements, where standard unary operations may not be sufficient.

Conclusion

In this chapter, we delved into the concept of simulating Object Oriented Programming using Lua tables. Although Lua is not inherently an object-oriented programming language, we discovered how tables can be utilized to create object-oriented-like structures. Throughout our exploration, we learned various techniques such as defining objects with tables, manipulating object properties, invoking object methods, and employing methods to construct and manipulate objects. Additionally, we explored the concept of encapsulation and how it can be achieved through the use of modules in Lua.

Metatables and metamethods emerged as powerful tools within Lua, enabling us to redefine how tables behave and handle operations such as addition, subtraction, and more. By harnessing the capabilities of metatables and metamethods, we can craft code that is more expressive and extensible. Specifically, we focused on the __add metamethod, which allowed us to override the addition operation and provided practical insights into performing matrix addition using metatables and metamethods. By incorporating these concepts into our programs, we can elevate Lua's capabilities and construct more sophisticated applications.

By leveraging Lua's robust table data structure, the convenience of the colon operator, the flexibility of methods, and the modular nature of Lua's modules, we can effectively simulate some object-oriented programming features and build highly adaptable applications.

Questions

1. What is object-oriented programming, and how does it organize code?

2. How can we create objects in Lua using tables?

3. What happens when we assign a table to another variable in Lua?

4. How can we invoke object methods in Lua?

5. What is the purpose of using methods in object-oriented programming?

6. How can we use modules to encapsulate objects in Lua?

7. What are metatables and metamethods in Lua?

8. How can we modify table behavior using metatables and metamethods?

9. What are some common metamethods in Lua, and how can we use them?

Exercises

1. Create a Lua table representing a car object with attributes like model, color, and mileage.

2. Assign the car table to another variable and modify one of its attributes. Print both variables to see if they reflect the changes.

3. Implement a method in the car object that increases the mileage by a given value. Test the method on your car object.

4. Create a Lua table representing a student object with attributes like name, age, and grade. Implement a method to print the student's information.

5. Create a Lua table representing a matrix object and define metamethods to handle matrix addition, subtraction, and multiplication. Test these operations on your matrix object.

Digging Deeper

You can learn more about Lua Metamethods at http://lua-users.org/wiki/MetatableEvents

Chapter 16: Next Steps

There are so many ways that Lua is used. From using Lua to embed within your game, to using community-created packages, to using Lua to create AI, Lua is incredibly powerful and flexible, and most frequently found as a scripting tool to enrich other software. Here are a few ways that you continue your Lua journey.

Embedding Lua in games

My first experience with Lua was using it within World of Warcraft back in the early 2000s. Soon after, I was creating mobile applications using Lua in Solar 2D (formerly Corona Labs). If you are creating a game that you plan to add DLC or hope to see your players mod, Lua just makes sense. We have included the links to help you get started with embedding Lua as a part of your game below for the two most popular game engines:

Unity
https://github.com/NLua/NLua

Unreal
https://github.com/rdeioris/LuaMachine

AI with Lua Torch

While Lua is not as commonly used in machine learning (ML) and artificial intelligence (AI) as Python, you can use Lua Torch to accomplish amazing machine learning feats. The Torch library is open source and provides all the tools you need to get started.

http://torch.ch/docs/getting-started.html#_

Lua Rocks

Lua (moon in Portuguese) Rocks (i.e. moon rocks) provides a package management for Lua. This enables the user to easily add new functions via modules created by other Lua developers. By using Lua Rocks in your Lua projects, you can streamline the process of adding external modules, tap into the Lua community's collective knowledge, and enhance the efficiency and functionality of your applications.

http://luarocks.github.io/luarocks/releases/.

Lua Bridge

LuaBridge is a lightweight and dependency-free library for mapping data, functions, and classes back and forth between C++ and Lua.

You can find more details and download the framework from
https://github.com/vinniefalco/LuaBridge

Additional Resources

If you would like to dig deeper into the Lua language, here are a few additional resources that I have found valuable.

The official definition of the Lua language is available on the Lua website https://lua.org. Reference manuals for the various releases of Lua are available at https://www.lua.org/manual/

Programming in Lua

by R. Ierusalimschy
Lua.org, fourth edition, August 2016
ISBN 8590379868
(also available as an e-book)
The official reference by Lua's chief architect, R. Ierusalimschy.

Lua Programming Gems

edited by L. H. de Figueiredo, W. Celes, R. Ierusalimschy,
Lua.org, December 2008
ISBN 9788590379843
(also available as e-book)

An older resource but still valuable collection of articles on the best practice on how to program in Lua

Other Recent Books

- ➢ Coding With Roblox Lua in 24 Hours: The Official Roblox Guide
  by Roblox Corporation. Sams Publishing, 2021, ISBN 9780136829423.
- ➢ Coding Roblox Games Made Easy: The ultimate guide to creating games with Roblox Studio and Lua programming
  by Zander Brumbaugh. Packt Publishing, 2021, ISBN 9781800561991.
- ➢ Developing Games on the Raspberry Pi: App Programming with Lua and LÖVE
  by Seth Kenlon. Apress, 2019, ISBN 9781484241707.
- ➢ Learning Mobile Application and Game Development with Solar 2D
  by Brian Burton. Burtons Media Group, 2019, ISBN 9781937336073

Lua-Oriented Websites

https://www.lua.org
The official site of the Lua scripting language.

http://lua-users.org/wiki/
A community of Lua users.

https://luarocks.org
Lua Rocks package manager

[Video Tutorials - Learning Lua on YouTube](#)
26 video tutorials on the Lua language by the author
of this book

Thank you for joining us on this journey of
Learning Lua!

Check out our newest books and resources at
BurtonsMediaGroup.com
YouTube.com/@profburton
https://discord.gg/tKSWMGh9fU

www.ingramcontent.com/pod-product-compliance
Lightning Source LLC
LaVergne TN
LVHW012334060326
832902LV00012B/1880